I0236103

Phil the PUG

Phil-osophy: Life According to a Pug

A Picture Book of Pug Wisdom, Snacks, and Snuggles

By Phil the Pug & Kaz Rance

Copyright © 2025 Kaz Rance & Phil the Pug (Kaz & Pug Press)

All rights reserved. No part of this publication may be reproduced, distributed, or transmitted in any form or by any means, including photocopying, recording, or other electronic or mechanical methods, without the prior written permission of the publisher, except in the case of brief quotations embodied in critical reviews and cert... contact:
philthepug@outlook.com

Cover design, photography, and illustrations by Kaz Rance
Phil's voice and emotional support by Phil the Pug

ISBN: 978-1068152726
Printed in United Kingdom
First Edition

This is a work of love, snorts, and emotional support. Any resemblance to other pugs, snacks, or life philosophies is purely coincidental—but probably delicious.

This book is intended to offer comfort, humour, and emotional support through the voice of Phil the Pug. It is not a substitute for professional mental health advice, diagnosis, or treatment. If you are struggling, please reach out to a qualified healthcare provider, therapist, or support service. You deserve care, and you are not alone.

Phil may be emotionally available, snack-fuelled, and deeply wise—but he is not a licensed therapist. He is, however, an excellent listener and a world-class napper.

💛 Dedication Page

To everyone who's ever needed a soft snort, a warm lap, and a reminder that they're doing just fine.

To my mum and dad—who are no longer here, who chose me, accepted me into their family, and whose love shaped me, and made me the person I am today. I carry them in every page, every snort, every step forward.

To Tina and Ezra—thank you for choosing me, accepting me, and loving me through every fault and every dark moment. You've given me the space to be my true self, and I'll never stop being grateful.

To Scrappy, my loyal son for 12 years. You paved the way for Phil and gave me the gift of unconditional love when I needed it most.

To David and Ali, Jane and Rod, thank you for your unwavering belief, support, and love. Always.

And to Phil—my muse, my anchor, my emotional support pug. You snorted me back to life and taught me how to rest with pride.

And finally, to you—the one holding this book. You are snack-worthy, loved, and never too much. This is your emotional support in hardback form.

✏️ Author's Note

There was a time I didn't know how to rest. I didn't know how to ask for help, or how to believe I was worthy of softness. Then came Phil—leather-clad, emotionally available, and full of snorts that somehow made everything feel okay.

This book is a love letter to that journey. To the quiet victories. To the blanket forts. To the snacks that saved us. It's for anyone who's ever felt too much, not enough, or just plain tired. You're not alone. You're not broken. You're beautifully bendy.

Phil taught me that emotional support doesn't have to be loud. Sometimes it's a warm lap, a knowing look, or a caption that makes you laugh through tears. I hope this book feels like that for you.

Thank you for being here. Thank you for choosing softness. And thank you for letting Phil and me walk beside you—even if we're wearing sunglasses indoors.

🐾 Phil's Welcome Page

Hi. I'm Phil. I'm a pug. I've got feelings, fashion, and a face that's been described as "emotionally available."

This book is my brain. Or at least the snack-fuelled, nap-loving, leather-jacket-wearing part of it. Inside, you'll find my thoughts on rest, resilience, snacks, and surviving the chaos with style.

I'm not a therapist. I'm just a pug who's seen some stuff. But if you need a reminder that you're doing okay—even if you cried in the fridge—I've got you.

Now grab a biscuit, get comfy, and let's snort our way through life together.

📝 Phil-osophy: Life According to a Pug

Table of Contents

🐾 **Chapter Eight: Phil's Guide to Good Hoomans** *Because some tail wags are earned. And some aren't*

🐾 **Chapter Nine: The Ethics of Ear Licks & Emotional Labour** *Affection is beautiful. But it's also effort. And effort deserves rest.*

🐾 **Chapter Ten: Love Me, Love My Wiggle** *Radical self-acceptance, tail-first*

🐾 **Chapter Eleven: Trust the Tail Wag** *Instincts. Gut Feelings. Emotional Radar. Phil knows.*

🐾 **Chapter Twelve: The Emotional Leash Agreement** *Boundaries, trust, and walking together—even when the lead is invisible*

🐾 **Bonus Section**

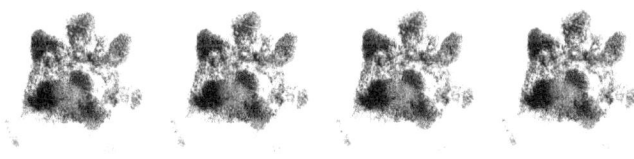

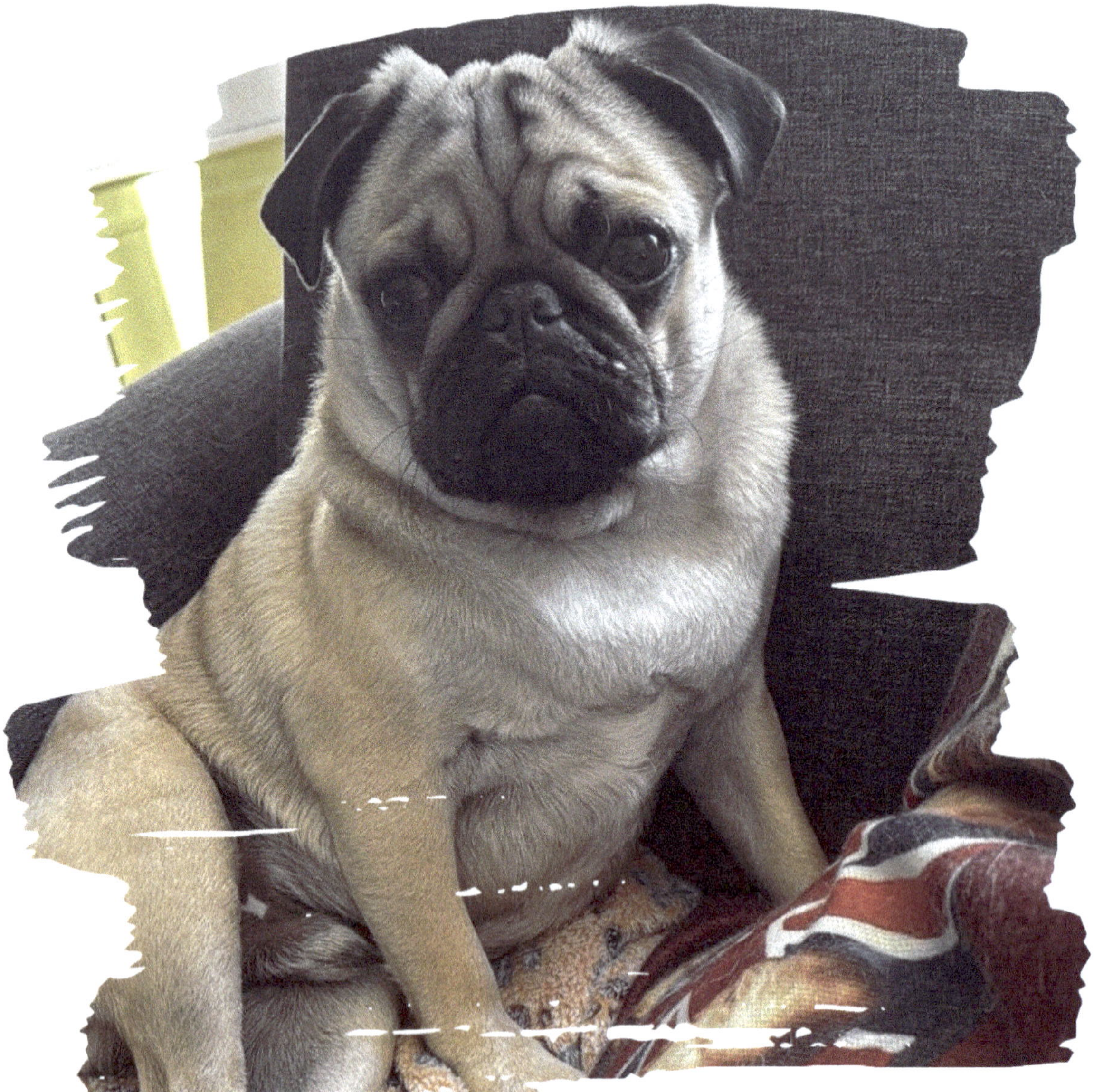

Chapter 1: Phil's Thoughts of Self-Worth

Because knowing your value is the first pug-powered glow-up

Welcome to Chapter One. The beginning. The snort that started it all.

This chapter is about knowing your worth—even when the world forgets to offer you a biscuit. It's about standing firm in your fur, even when the blanket's been stolen.

You are enough. You are snort-worthy. And you don't need anyone else to validate your tail wiggle.

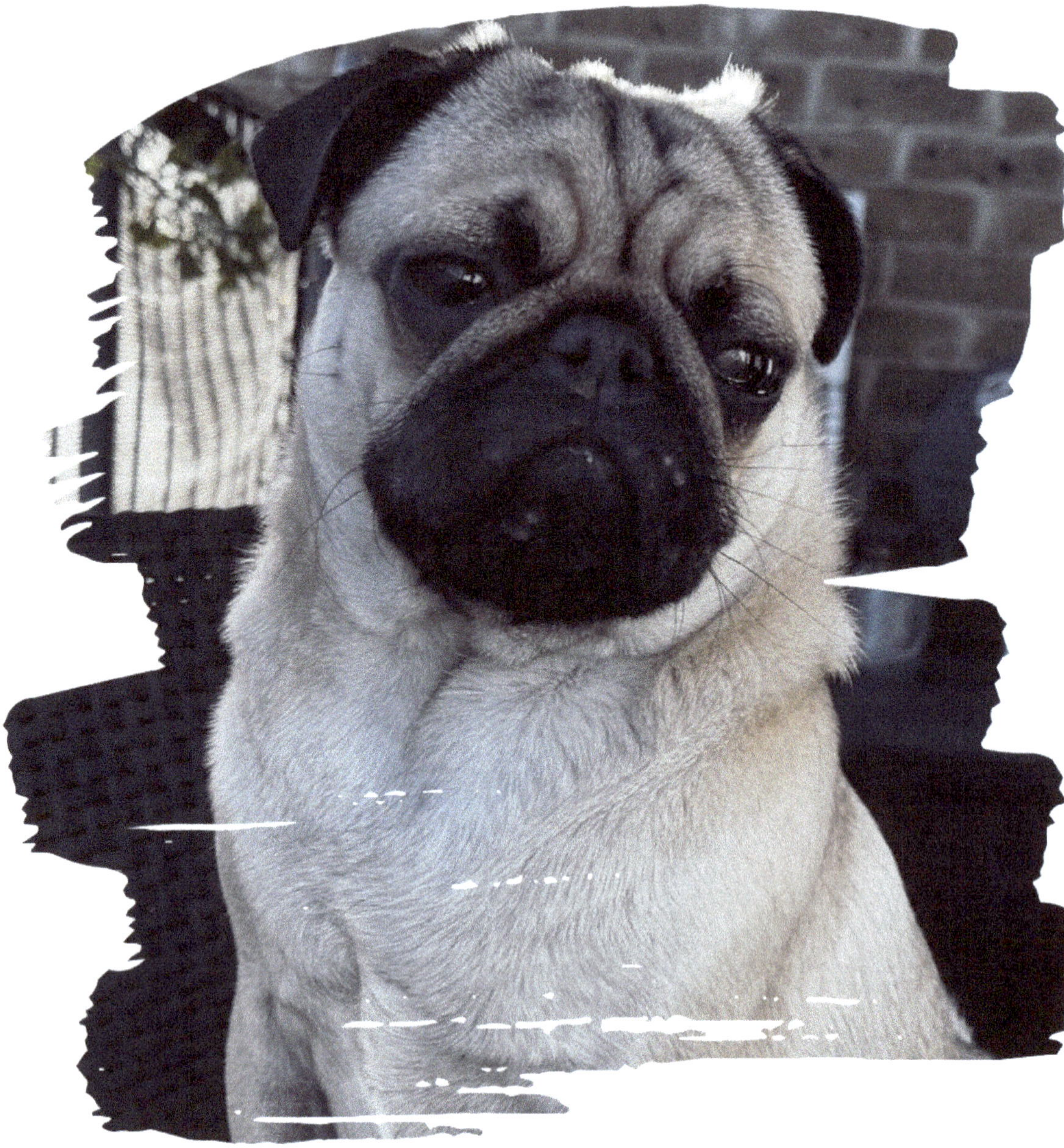

The Thought of Enough Ness

Phil-osophical Quote:

"You don't have to earn love. You just have to be."

Phil-osophy in Practice:

I used to think I had to do tricks for treats. Sit for snuggles. Be quiet to be loved. But then I realised: I am enough. Even when I snort too loud. Even when I steal socks. You are too. You don't have to perform to be worthy.

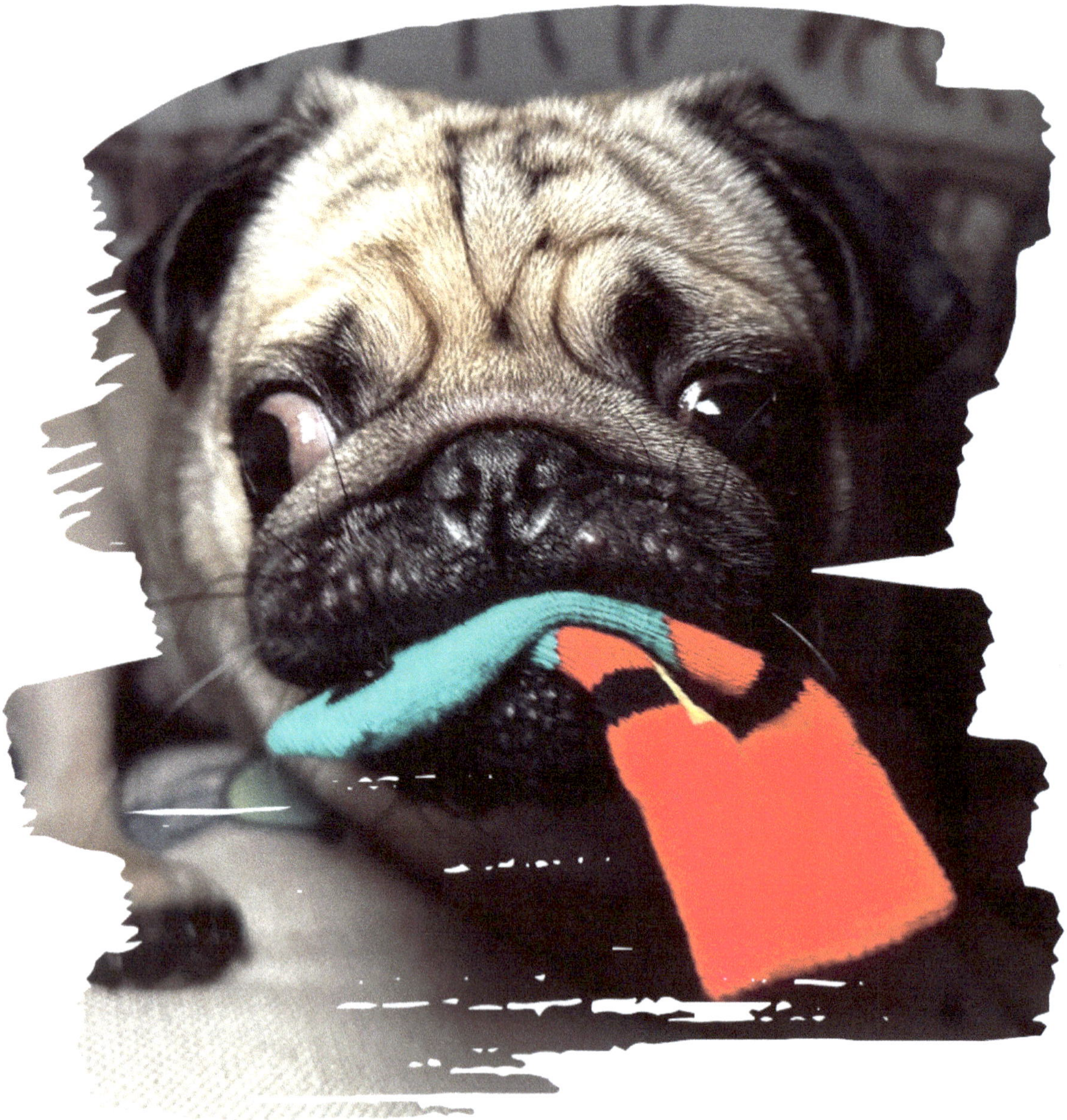

The Sock-Stealing Confidence

Phil-osophical Quote:

"Confidence is stealing the sock and not apologising."

Phil-osophy in Practice:

I don't steal socks because I'm naughty. I steal them because they smell like love. Confidence isn't loud. It's knowing you belong—even when you're holding a stolen sock in your mouth. You don't have to be perfect. You just have to be real.

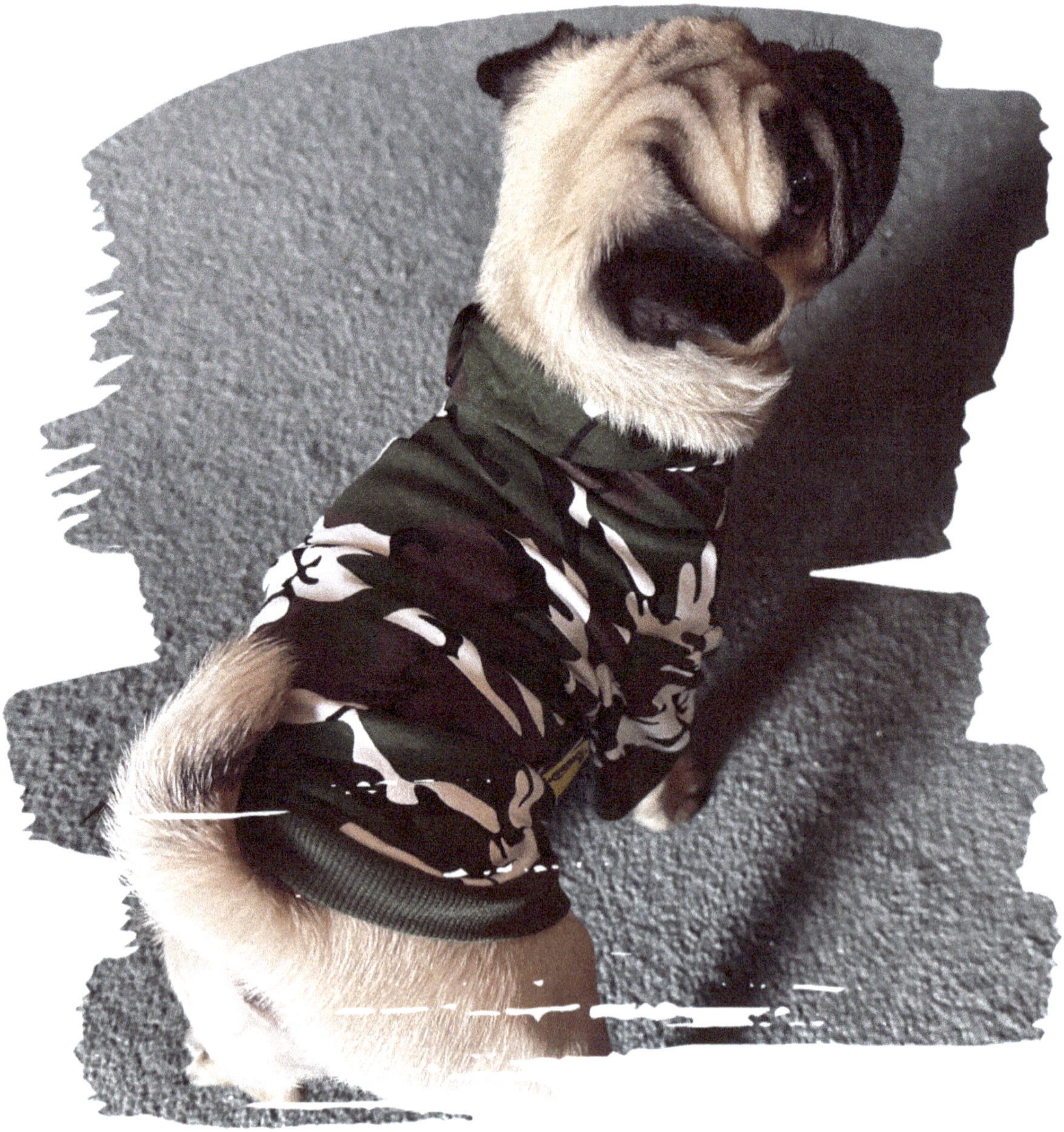

The Tail Wiggle of Worth

Phil-osophical Quote:

"Your tail wiggle is enough. Even when no one's watching."

Phil-osophy in Practice:

I wiggle my tail when I'm happy. When I'm hopeful. When I'm just existing. It's not for show. It's for me. Celebrate your tail wiggle moments. They're proof you're alive and worthy.

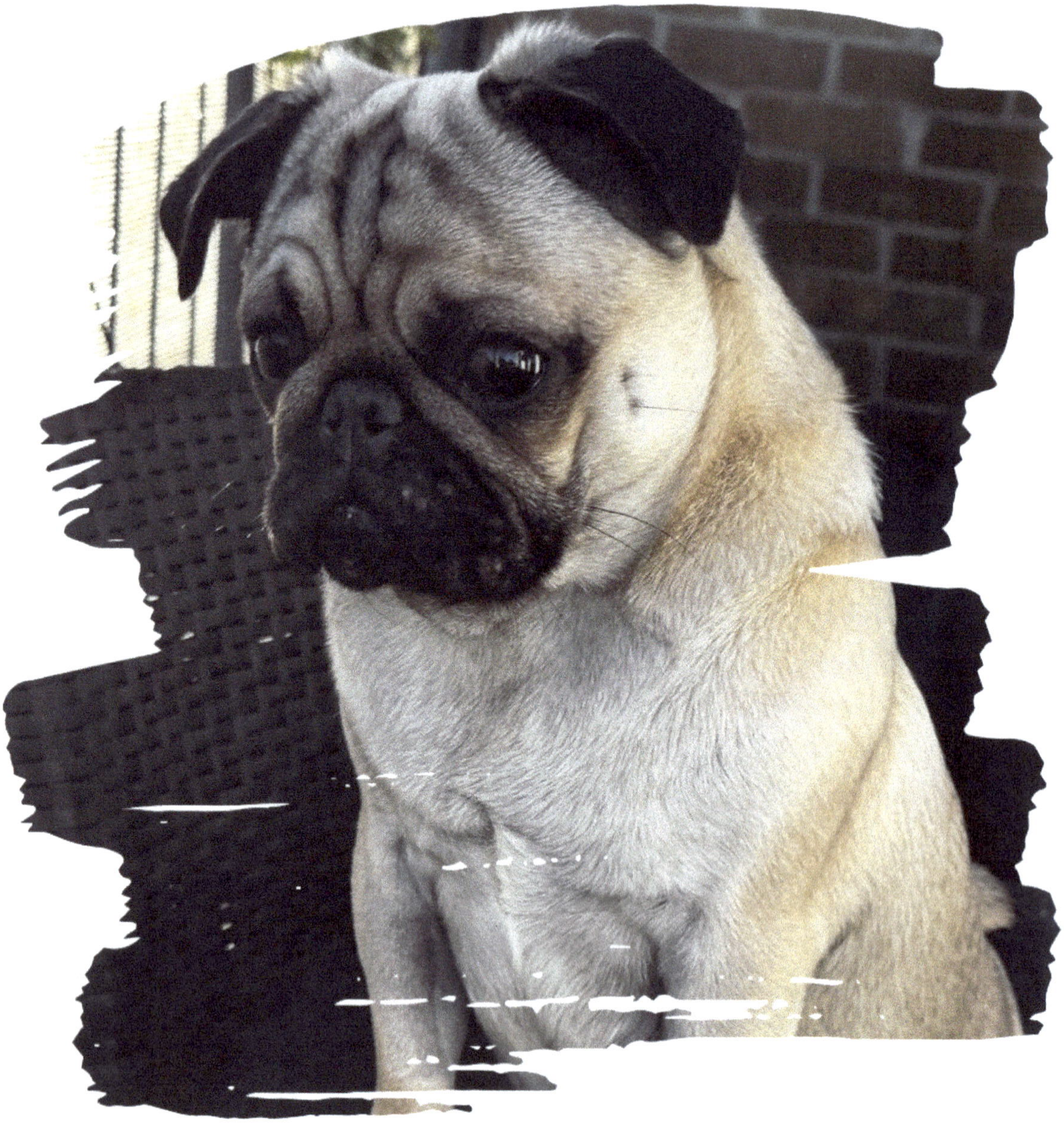

The Snort of Self-Respect

Phil-osophical Quote:

"If they don't respect your snort, they don't deserve your cuddle."

Phil-osophy in Practice:

I snort loudly. I snort often. And I won't apologise for it. Your quirks are part of your magic. Don't shrink them for anyone. Respect starts with accepting your own snort.

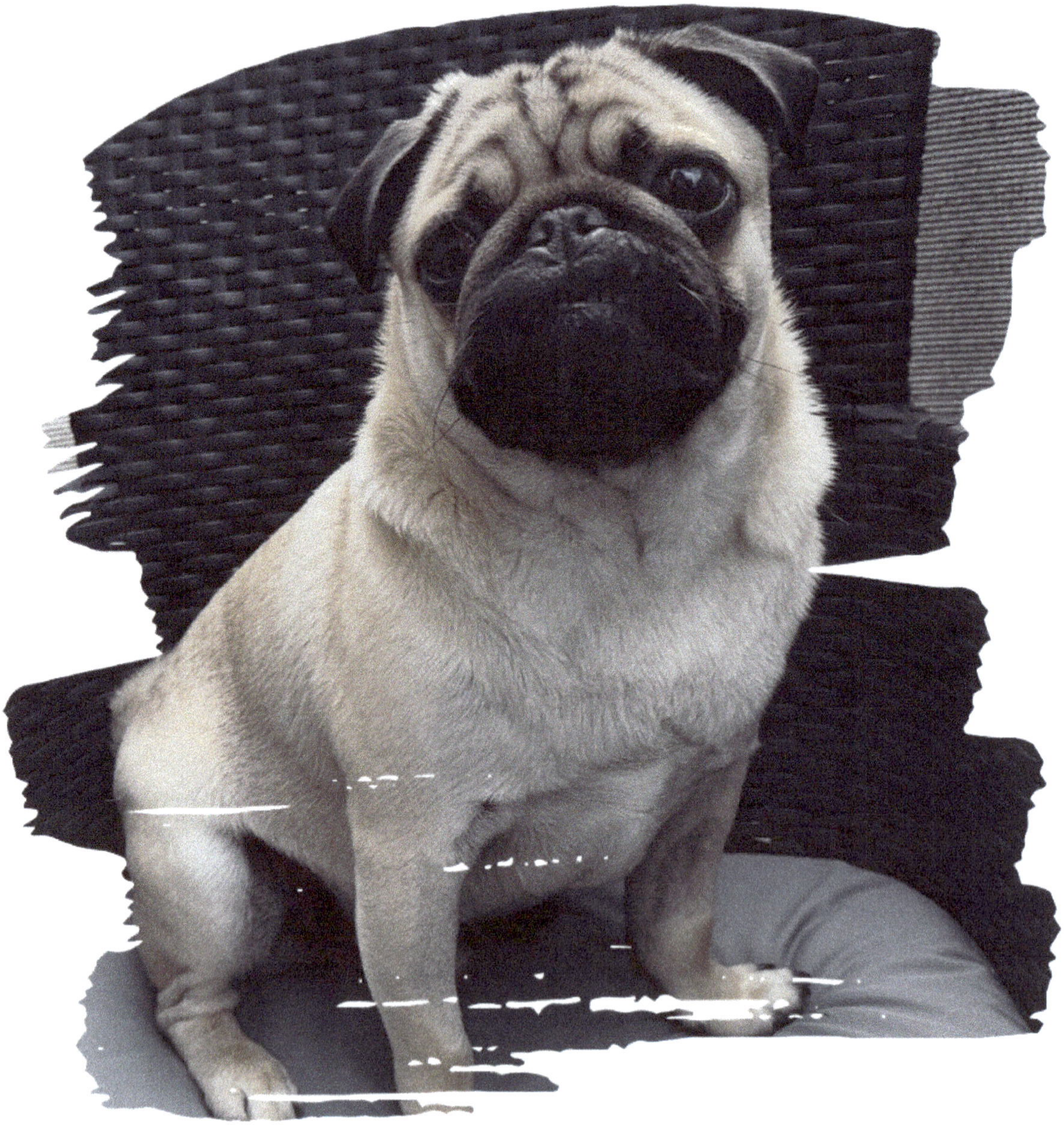

🧠 Phil's Final Pawse

Phil-osophical Quote:

"You are worthy. Even when the blanket's gone. Even when the biscuit's missing. Even when you snort too loud."

Phil-osophy in Practice:

This chapter is your reminder: you don't have to be quiet, small, or perfect to be loved. You are enough. You are snort-worthy. And you always have been.

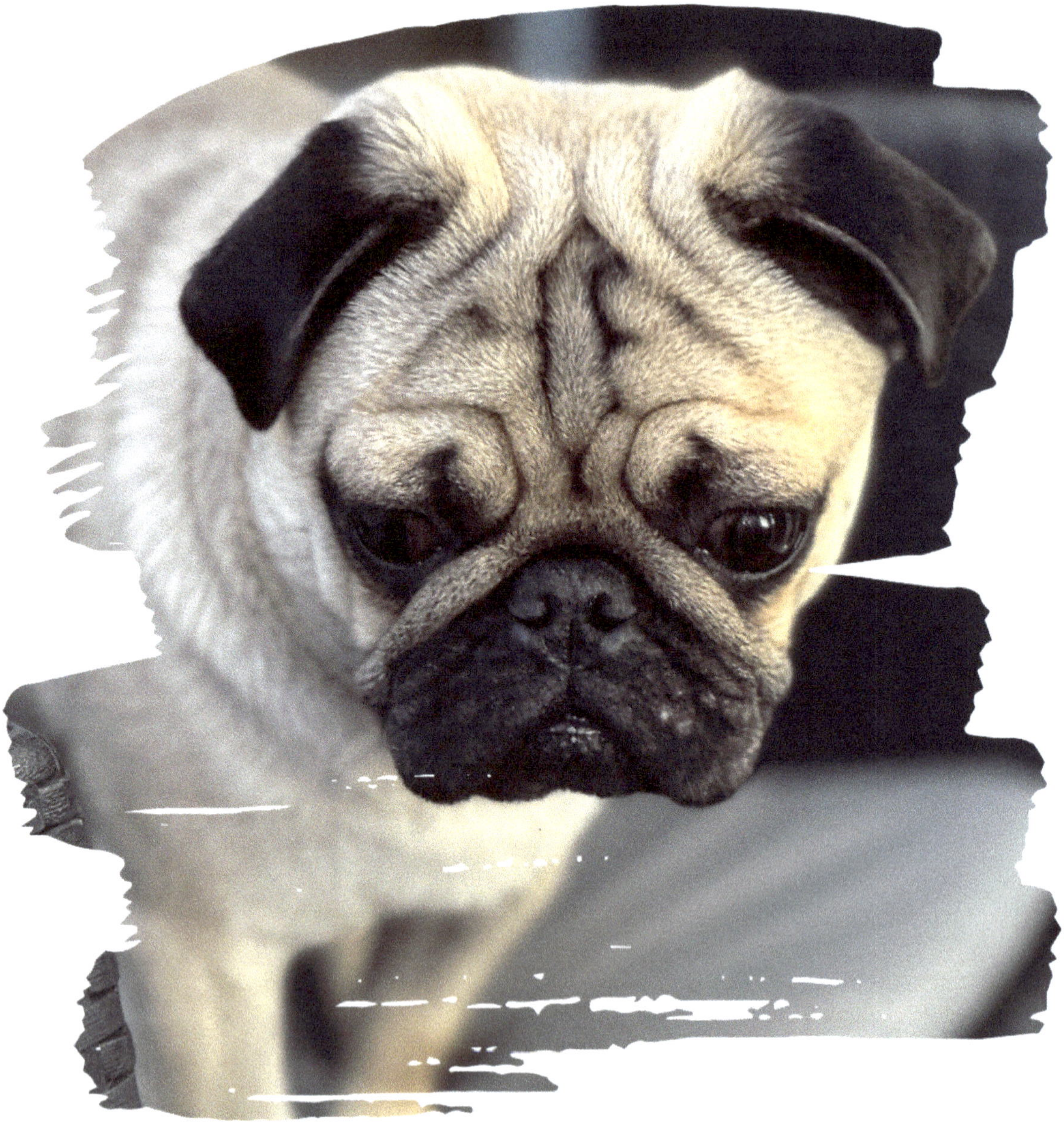

Chapter 2: The Art of Doing Nothing

Because rest isn't lazy – it's legendary

Welcome to Chapter Two. Or as I call it: The Ministry of Naps.

Here, we don't hustle. We don't grind. We don't even fetch unless it's emotionally fulfilling.

Phil-osophical Quote:

"Doing nothing is doing something. It's called healing."

Phil-osophy in Practice:

This chapter is about blanket forts, sunbeam therapy, and the radical act of doing absolutely nothing. If anyone tells you rest is lazy, bark softly and walk away. You're healing. You're conserving emotional energy. You're being a pug. If you've ever felt guilty for resting, I'm here to snort that guilt away.

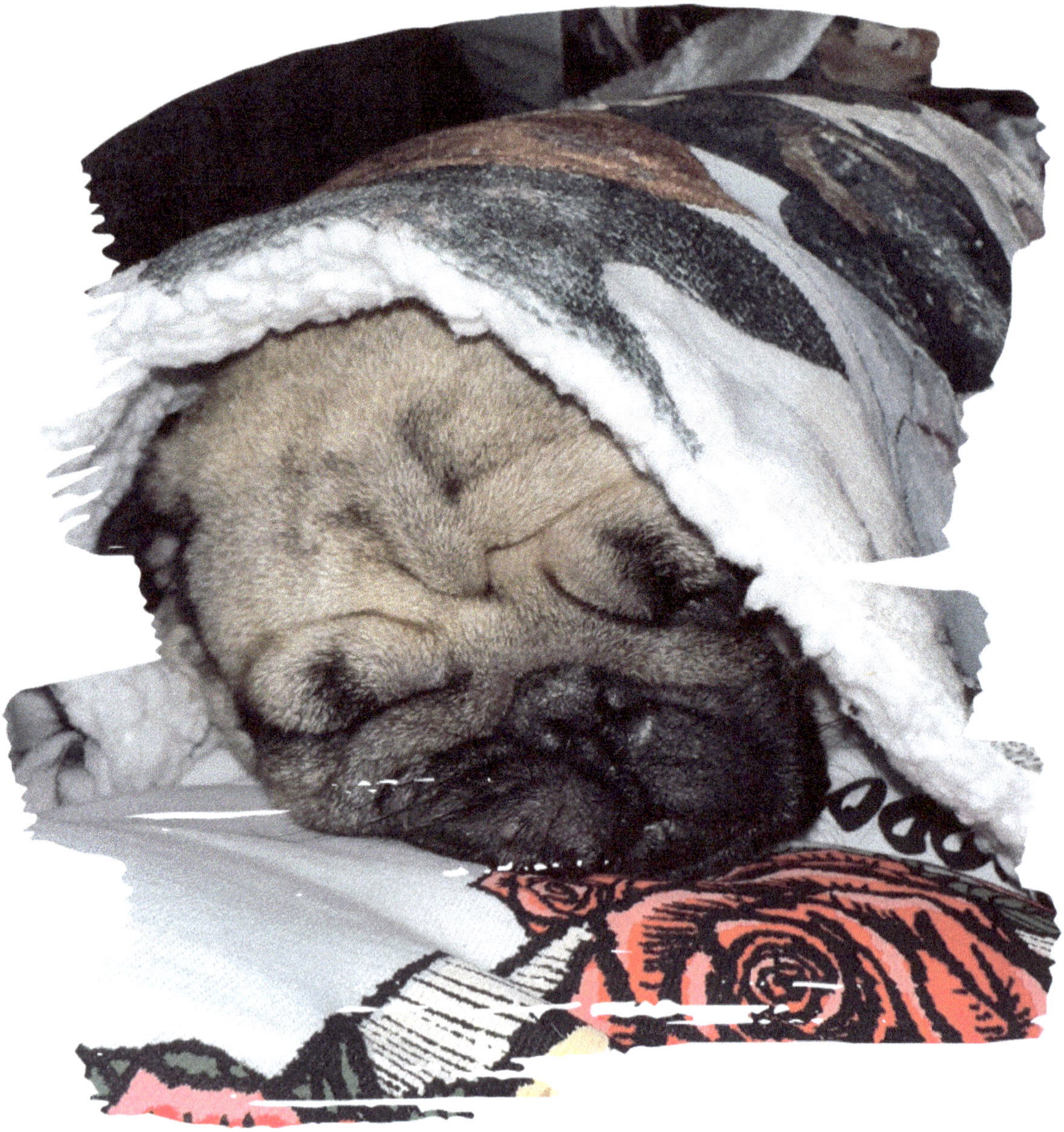

Blanket for Zen

Phil-osophical Quote:

"I'm not hiding. I'm healing. Also, it's warm in here."

Phil-osophy in Practice:

Some days, the world is loud. So, I build a fort. Not to escape—but to remind myself that softness is strength. You don't have to be productive to be powerful. You just need a blanket, a biscuit, and a bit of peace. Bonus points if the blanket smells like your hooman.

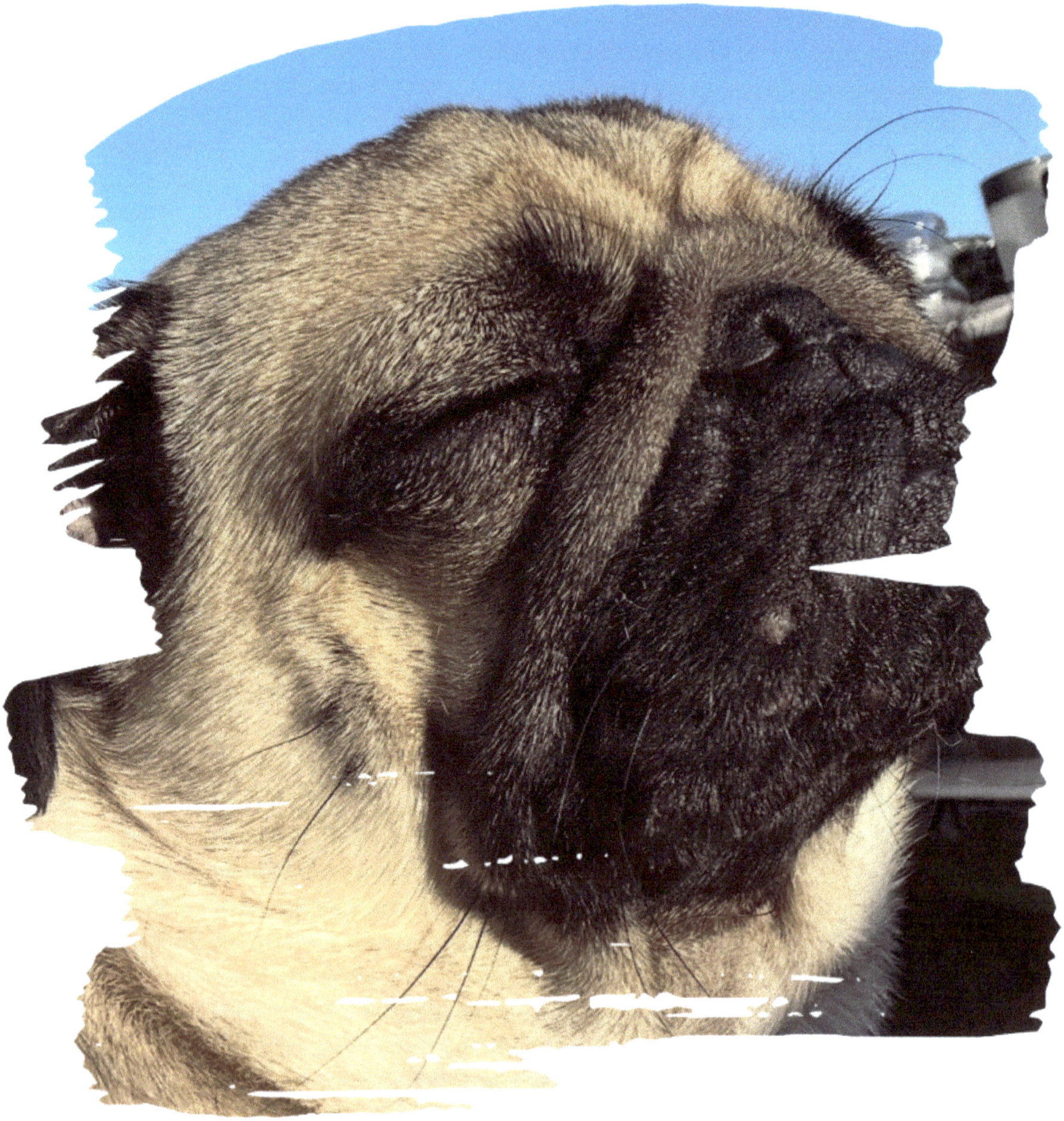

Sunbeam Therapy

Phil-osophical Quote:

"This is my therapy session. It's warm. It's free. And I don't have to talk about my childhood."

Phil-osophy in Practice:

I nap like it's my job. Because it is. I don't wait until I'm burnt out—I lie down pre-emptively. You don't have to earn rest. You just must claim it. Preferably in a sunbeam. Preferably with snacks nearby. And if someone interrupts you? Roll over dramatically and sigh.

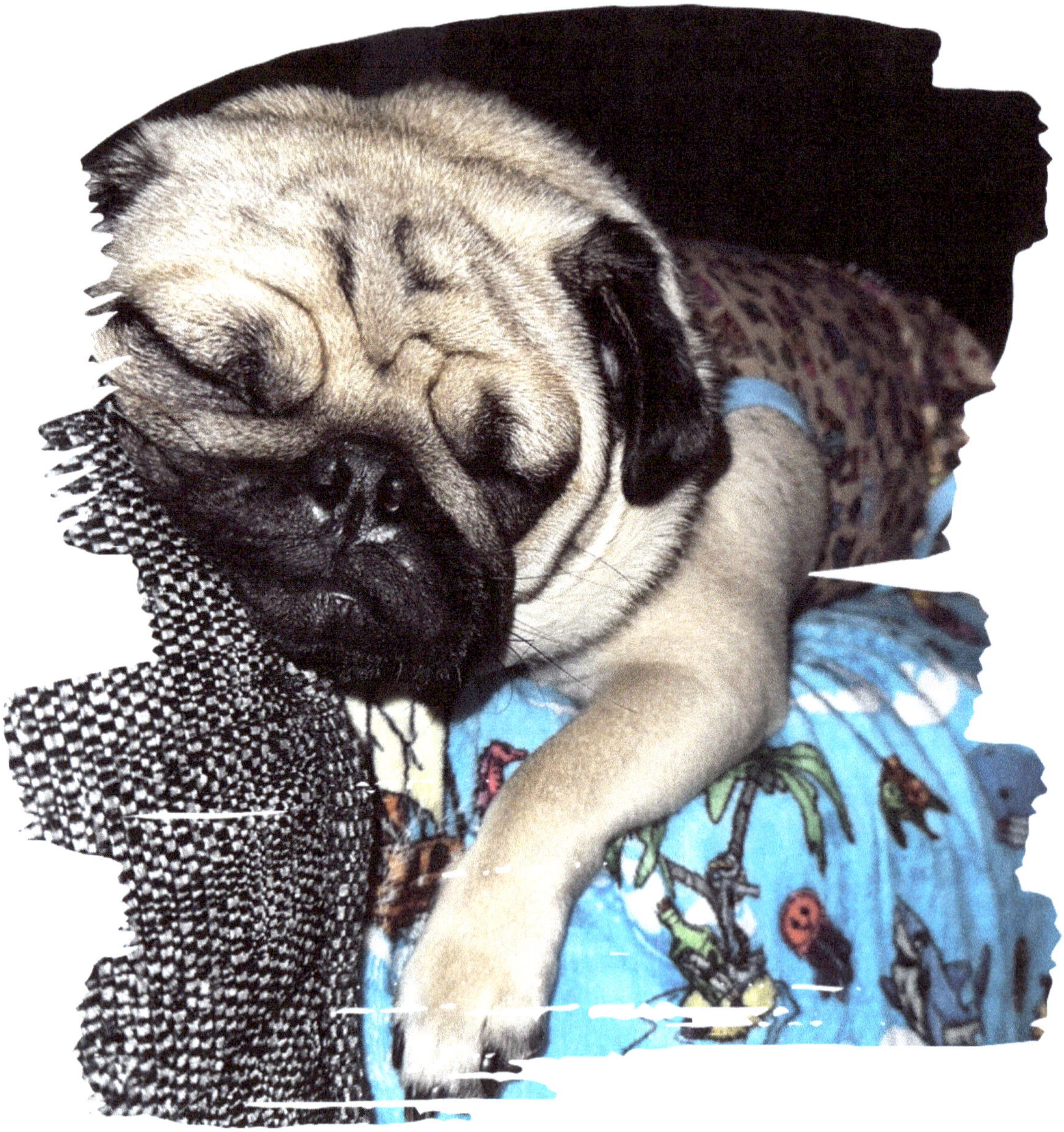

Emotional Energy Conservation

Phil-osophical Quote:

"I'm not ignoring you. I'm conserving emotional energy."

Phil-osophy in Practice:

Sometimes I choose silence. Sometimes I choose stillness. Sometimes I choose not to bark at the vacuum. That's not weakness. That's wisdom. That's pug-level emotional maturity. You don't have to react to everything. You're allowed to protect your peace—even if it means pretending you didn't hear the doorbell.

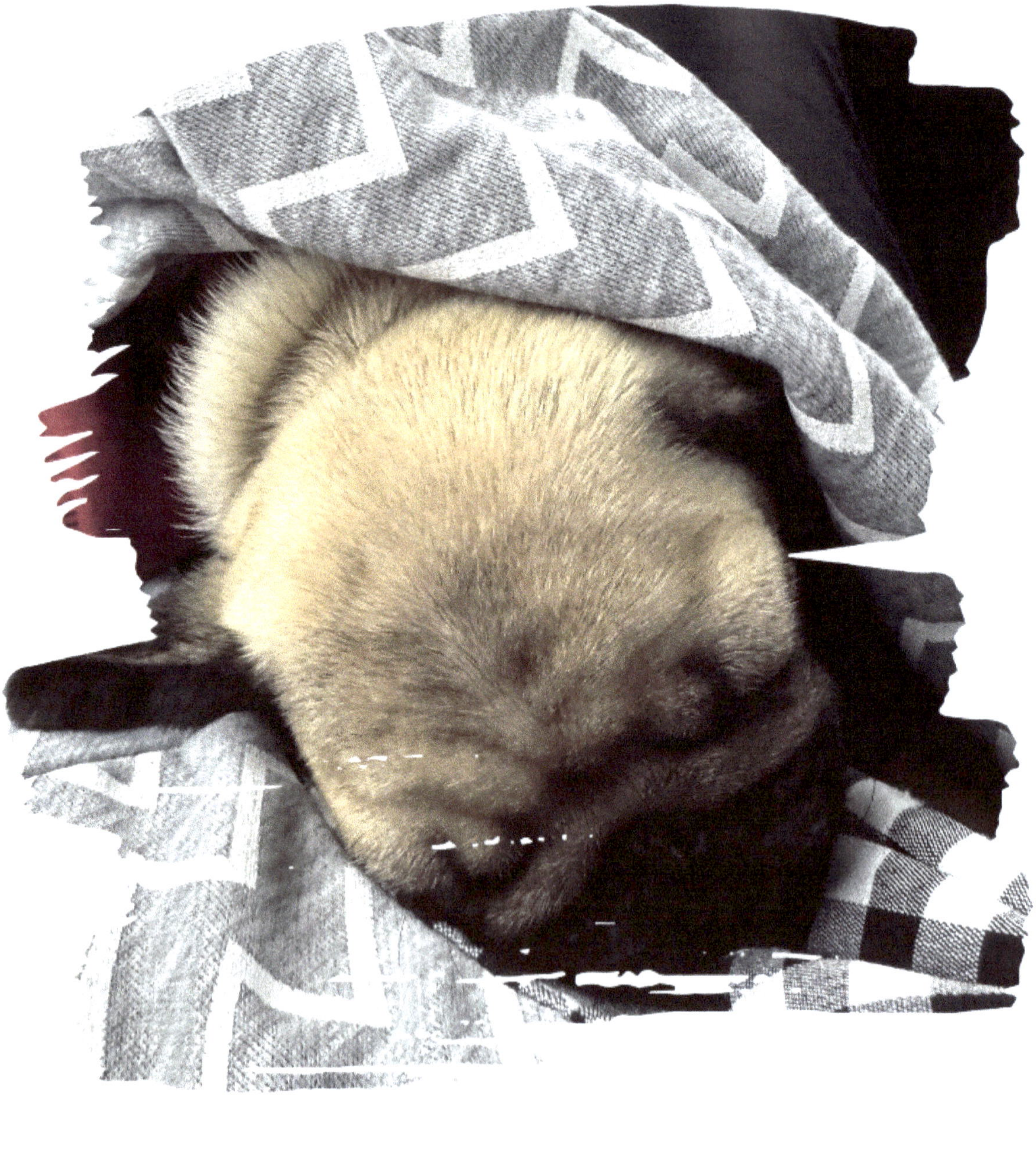

🧠 Phil's Final Pawse

Phil-osophical Quote:

"Doing nothing is doing something. It's called healing."

Phil-osophy in Practice:

You are allowed to rest. You are allowed to do nothing. You are allowed to exist without producing. I approve this message. Now go lie down. Preferably with a biscuit.

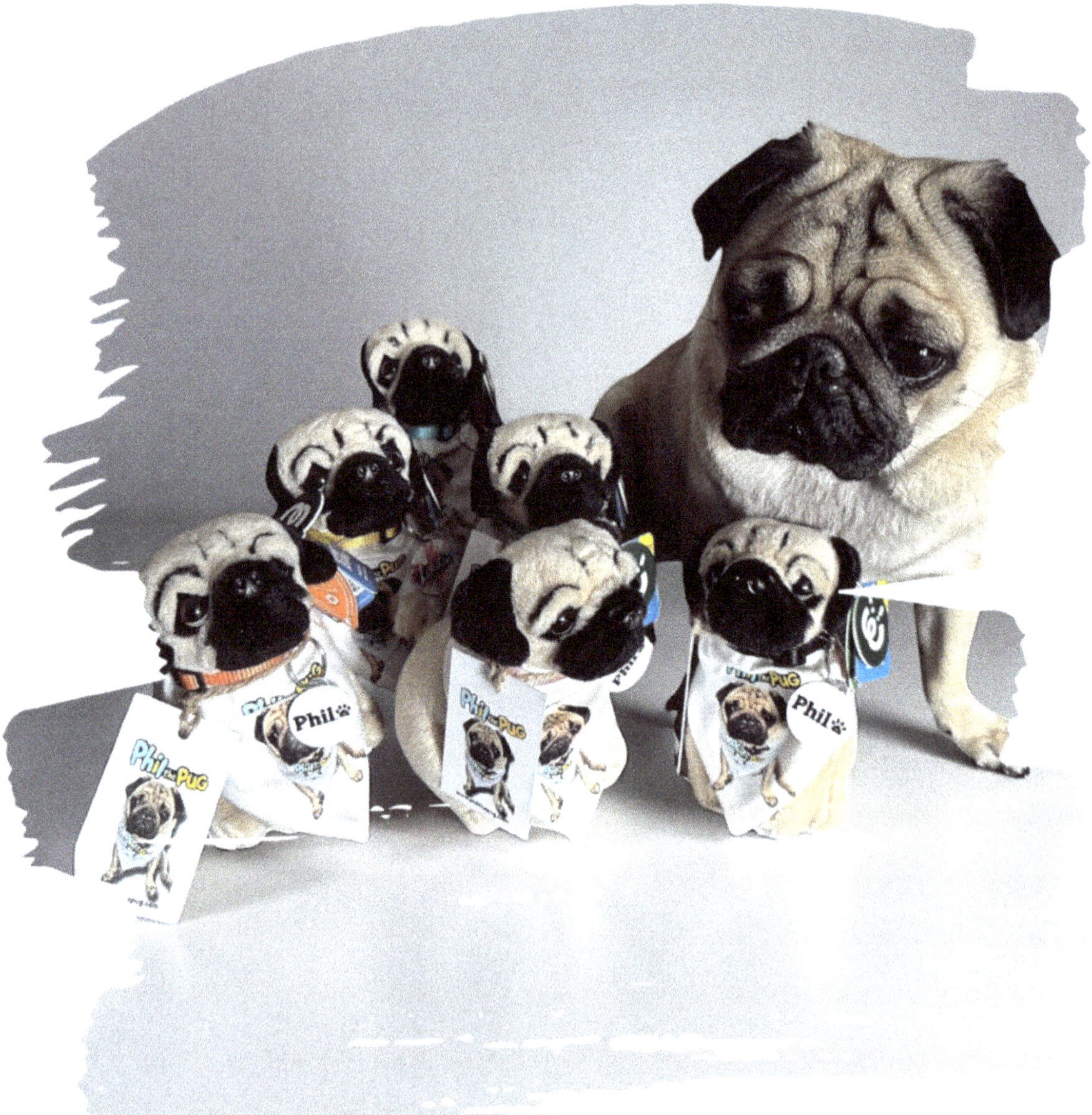
Phil
Phil
Phil

🍪 Chapter 3: Emotional Nourishment & Boundary Biscuits

Because you deserve the whole biscuit, not just crumbs

Welcome to Chapter three. Or as I call it, The Biscuit Worthy. Here, we don't settle for crumbs. We don't chase approval. We don't accept biscuits with emotional strings attached.

This chapter is about knowing your value, choosing nourishing snacks (literal and emotional), and remembering that you're not too much—you're a whole snack. With icing. And sprinkles. And maybe a second one for later.

If someone makes you feel small, bark gently, take your biscuit, and walk away with dignity. You're snack-worthy. You're loved. You're being a pug.

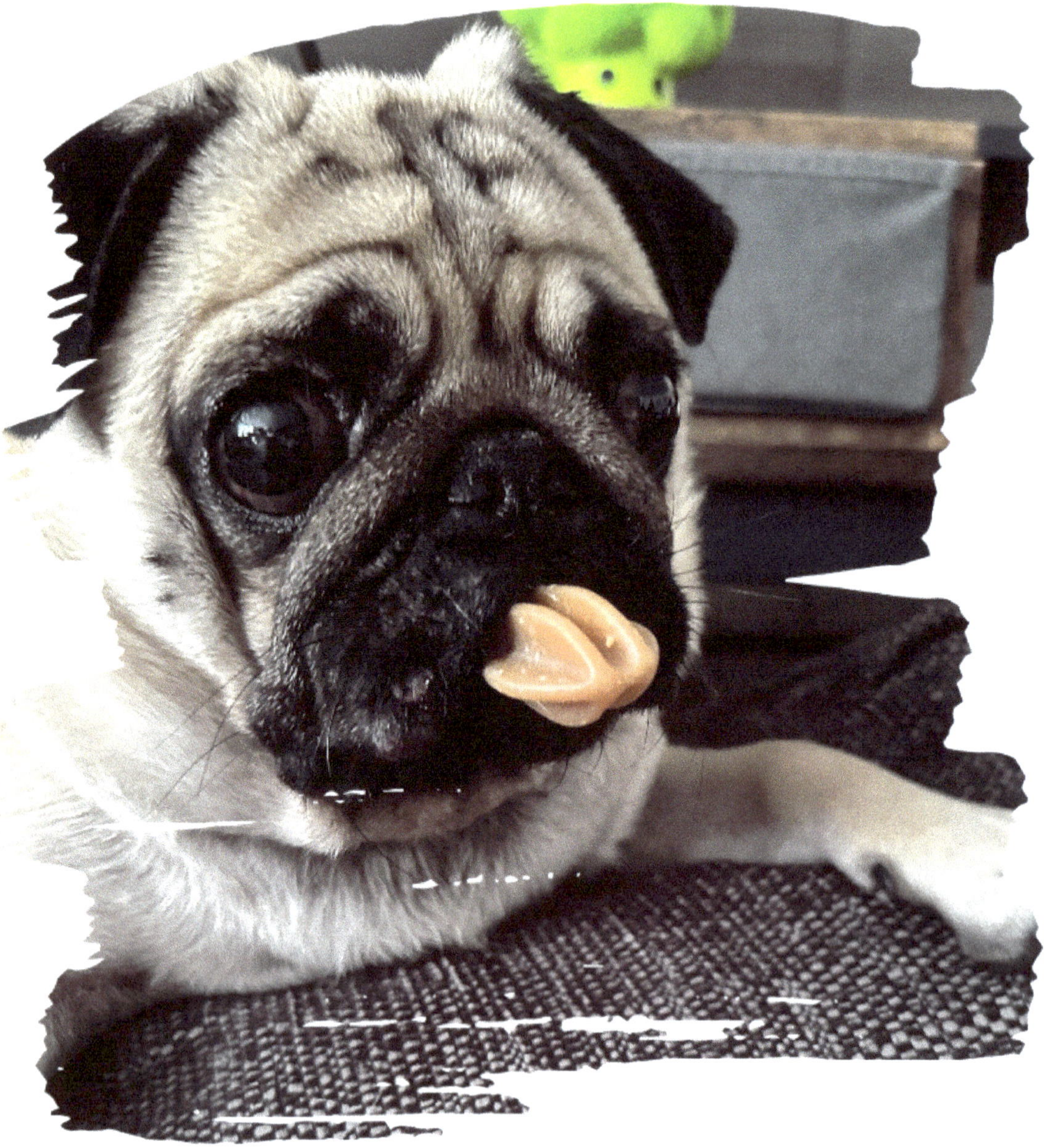

The Biscuit Test

Phil-osophical Quote:

"If they wouldn't share their biscuit with you... rethink the friendship."

Phil's Snack Reflections:

The Biscuit Test is simple: if they offer comfort, kindness, and snacks without making you beg—you've found a good one. If they guard their biscuit like it's gold and you're not worthy? Bark politely and move on. You're not a crumb. You're the whole snack.

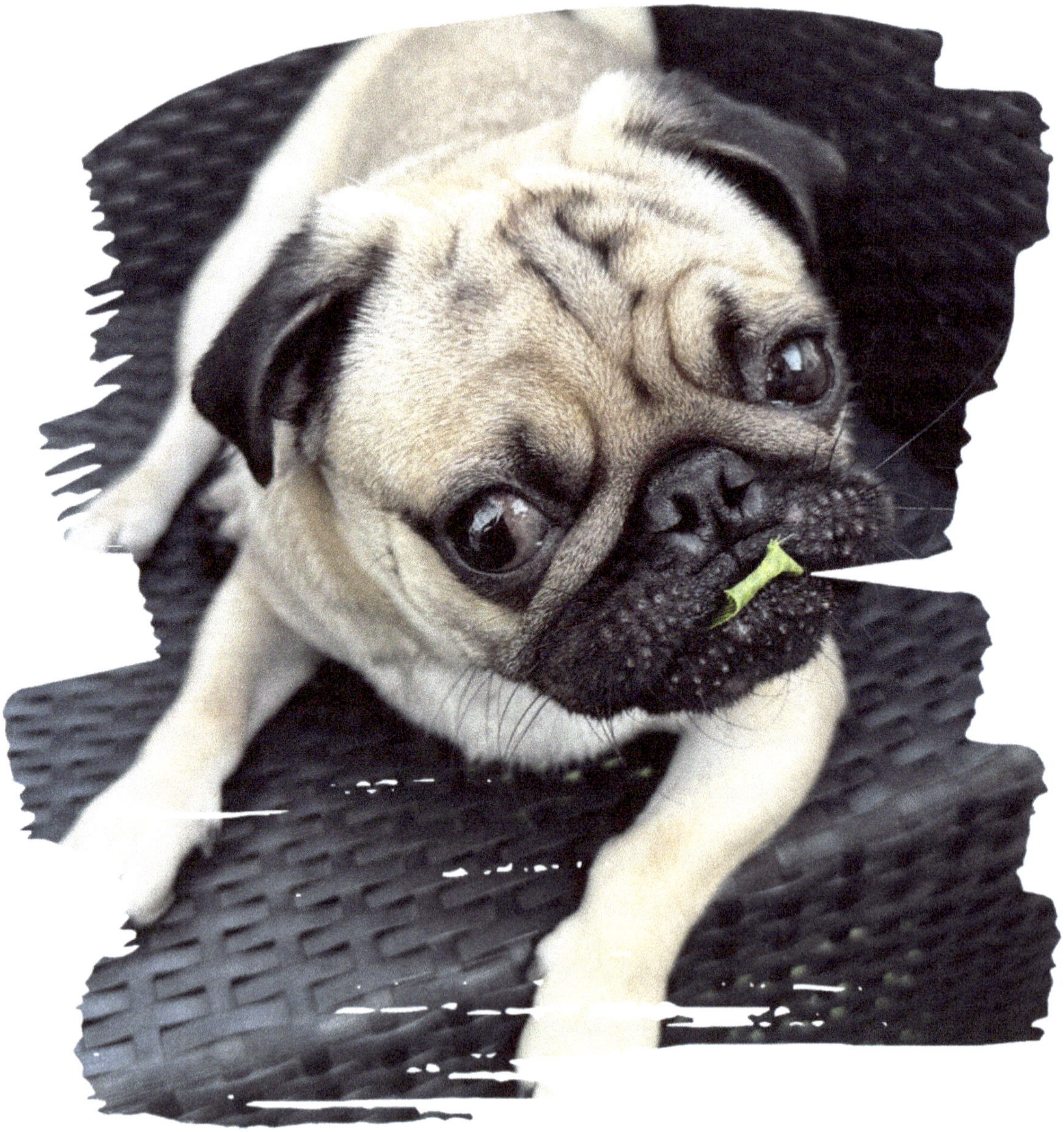

Snack Boundaries

Phil-osophical Quote:

"You can say no. Even to snacks. Especially to snacks that don't feel good."

Phil's Snack Reflections:

Not every snack is worth it. Some come with strings. Some make your tummy twist. You're allowed to say no. You're allowed to choose snacks—and people—that nourish you. That's called self-worth. That's called pug wisdom.

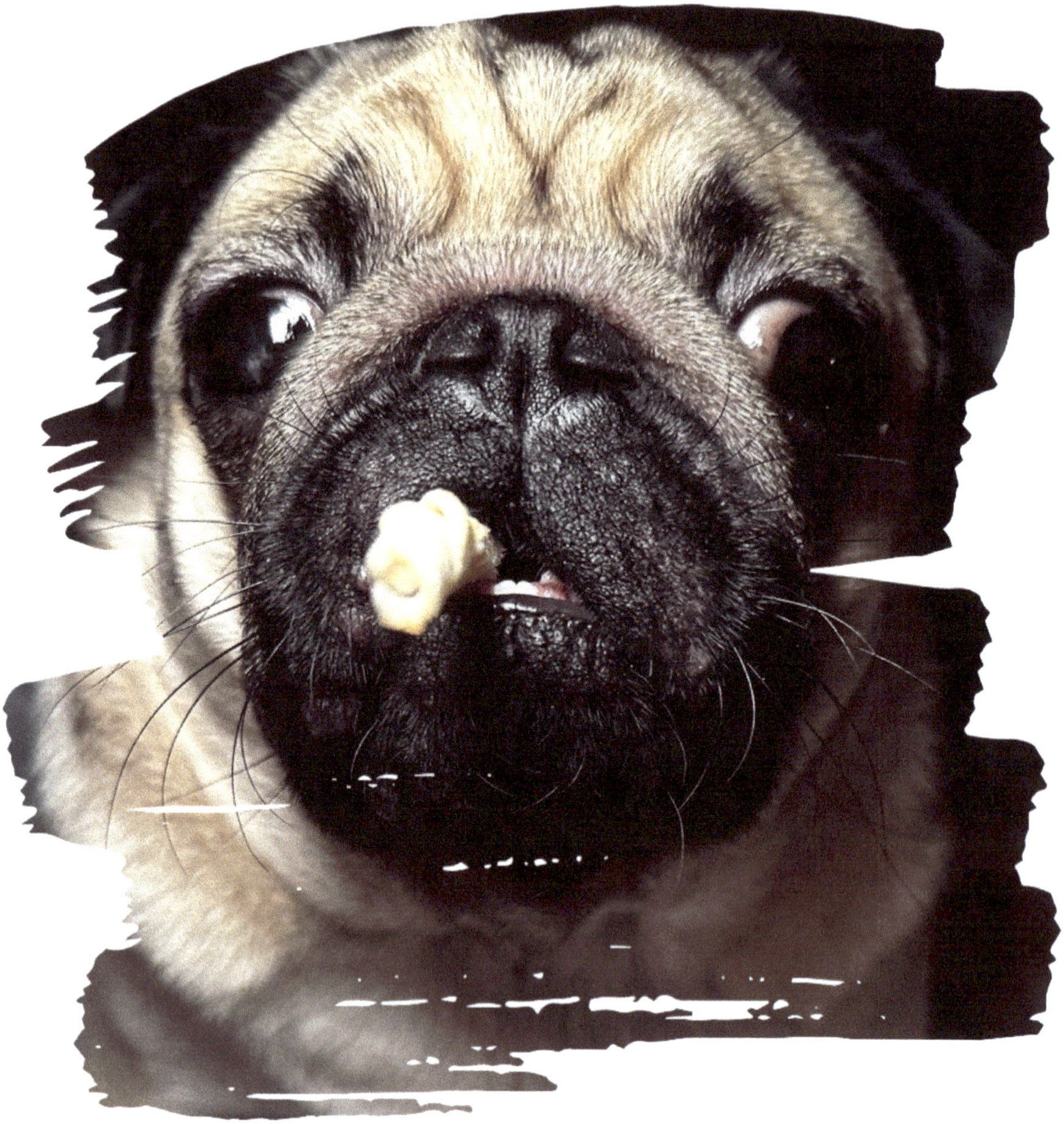

Snack Affirmations

Phil-osophical Quote:

"I am snack-worthy. I am loved. I am not too much."

Phil's Snack Reflections:

Say it with me: I am snack-worthy. I am loved. I am not too much. Say it in the mirror. Say it in the blanket fort. Say it while holding a biscuit. Because it's true. And because sometimes, you need to hear it from a pug.

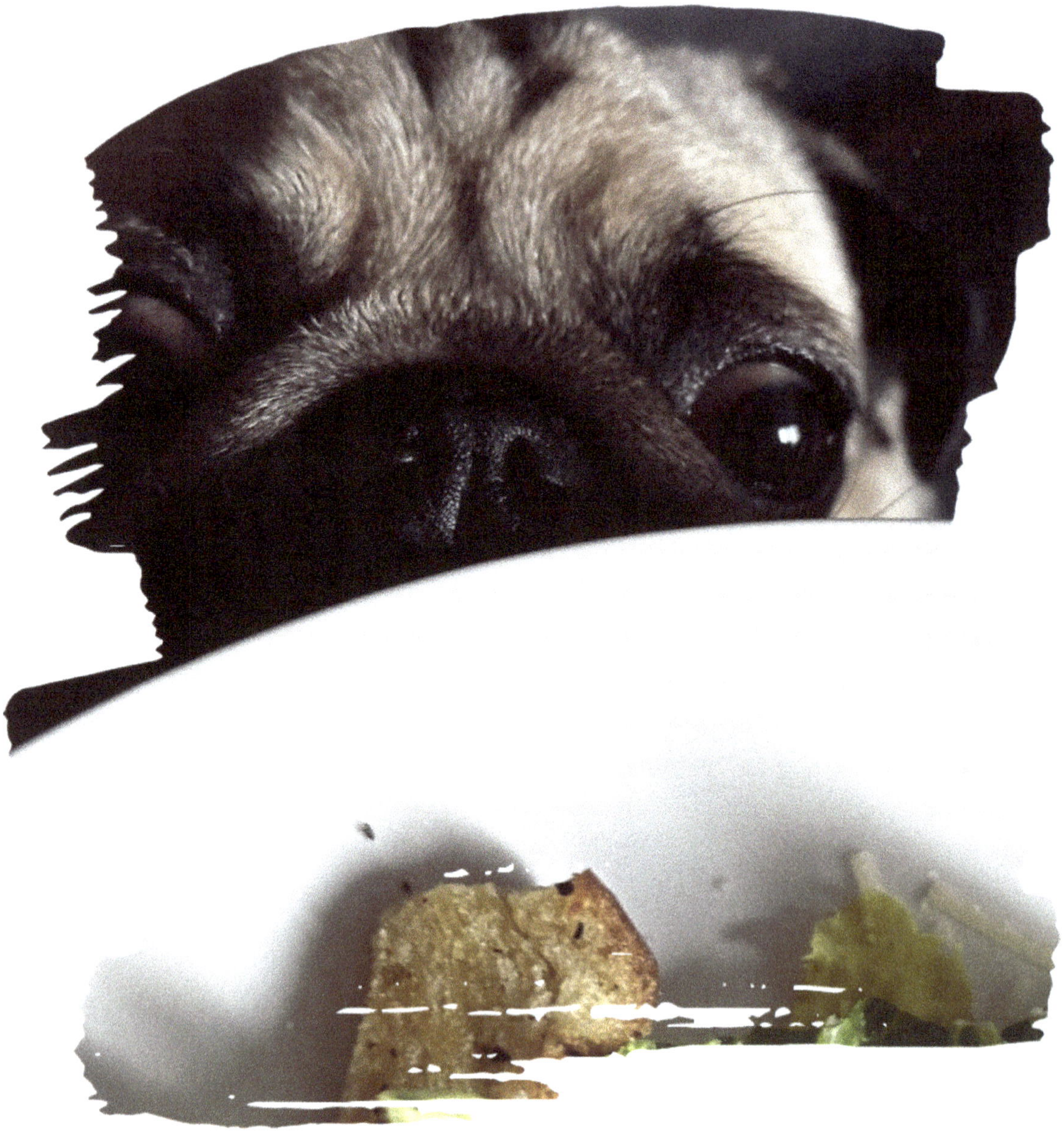

Snack Economics

Phil-osophical Quote:

"Snack wisely. Love generously. Nap often."

Phil's Snack Reflections:

Snacks are currency. But love is the real wealth. Don't trade your peace for approval. Don't give away your last biscuit to someone who wouldn't do the same. You're allowed to keep some for yourself. That's not selfish. That's self-care.

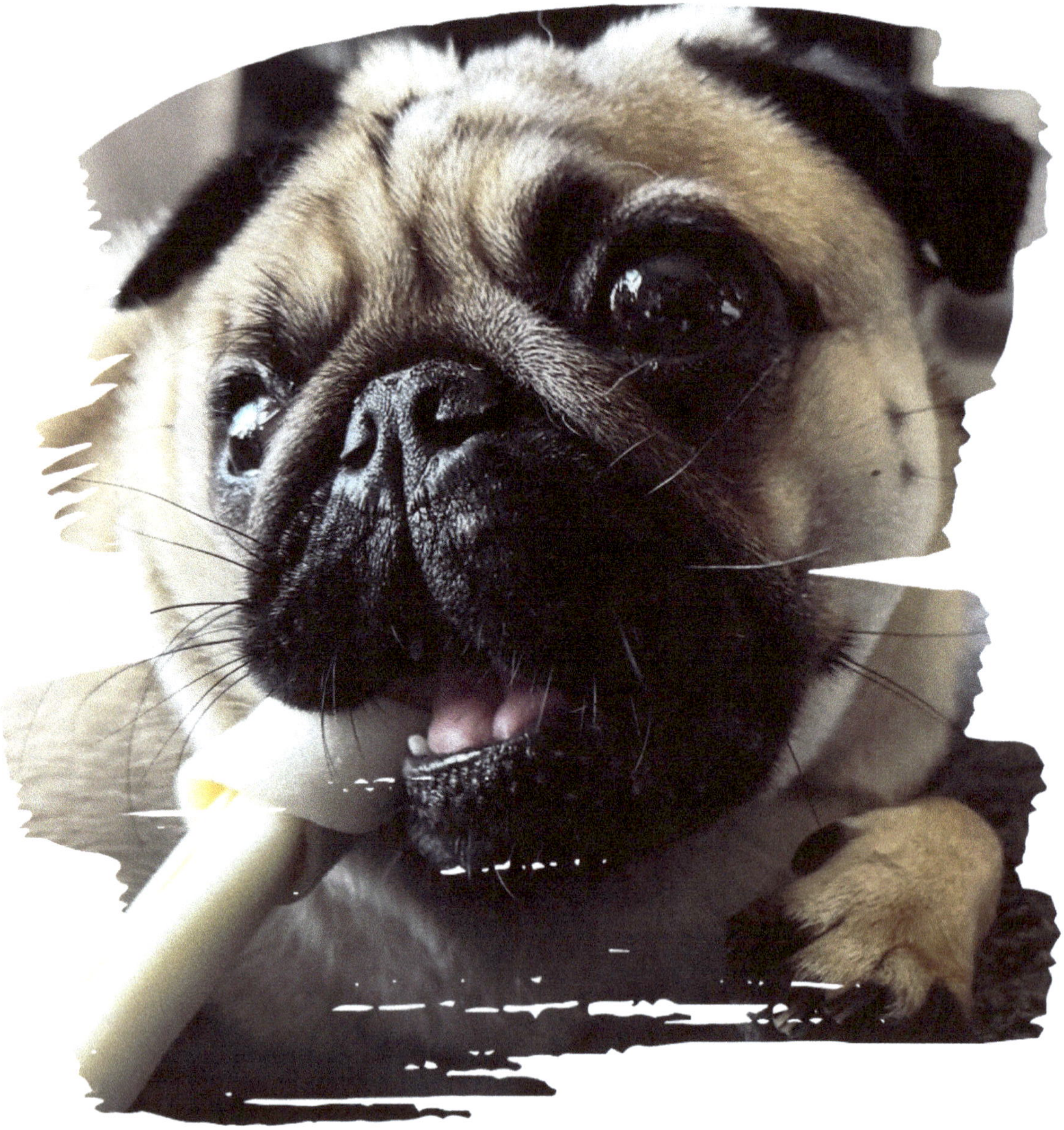

🧠 Phil's Final Pawse

Phil-osophical Quote:

"You are not a crumb. You are the whole snack."

Phil's Snack Reflections:

You are worthy of love, softness, and second helpings. You don't have to shrink to fit. You don't have to beg for crumbs. You are snack-worthy. You are enough. You are being a pug.

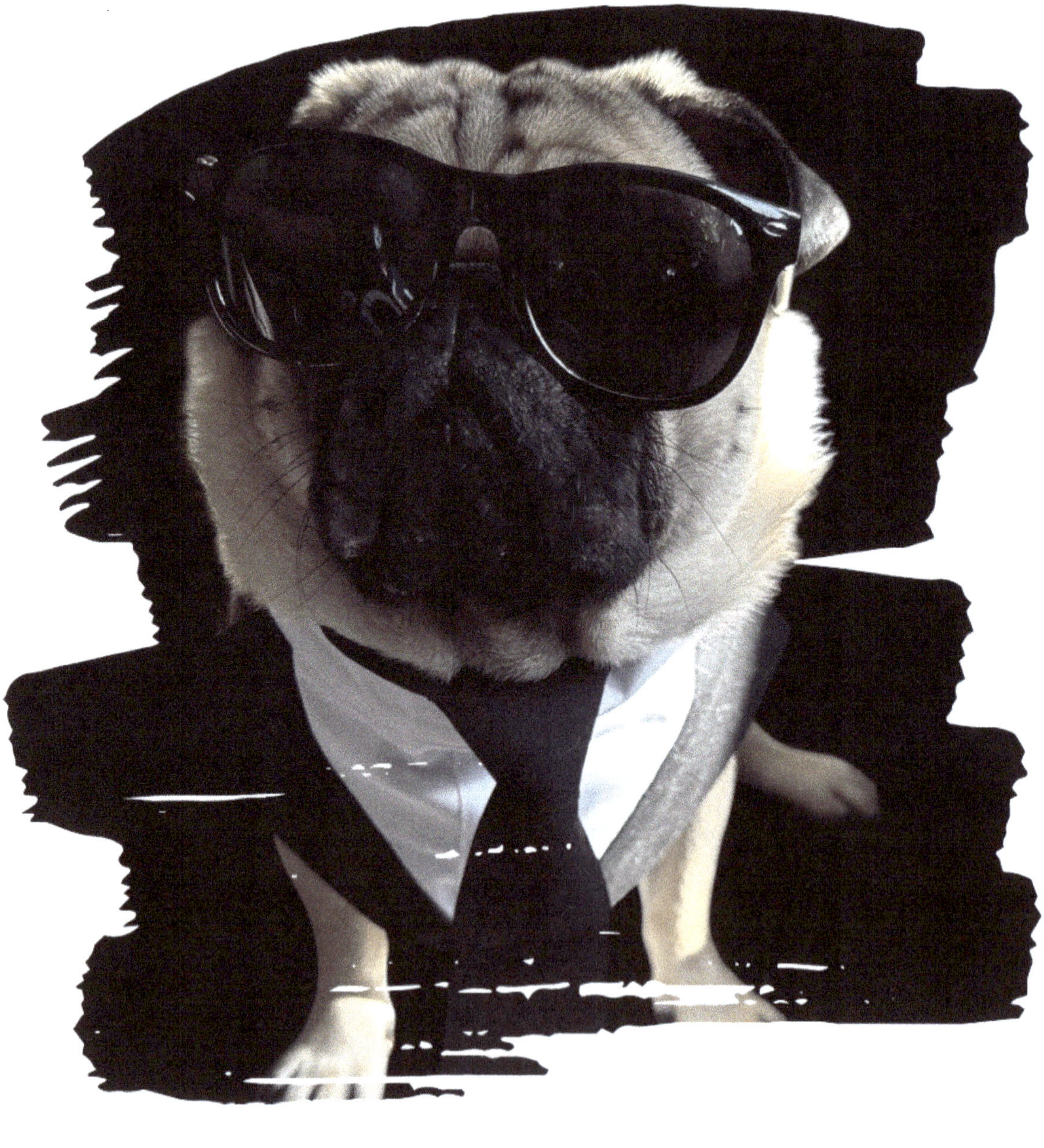

👗 Chapter 4: Fashion Is Feelings

Because sometimes the leather jacket says what the snort can't.

Welcome to Chapter Four. Or as I call it: The Ministry of Mood-Based Outfits.

Here, we dress for the drama. For the softness. For the snack run. For the emotional arc of the day.

Fashion isn't just fabric. It's feelings. It's identity. It's a way of saying "I'm here, I'm healing, and yes, this is a velvet cape."

Some days I wear leather. Some days I wear fluff. Some days I wear nothing but confidence and a biscuit crumb on my chin. All valid.

This chapter is about dressing how you feel, how you want to feel, and sometimes just for the joy of being seen. You're allowed to sparkle. You're allowed to wear the tutu. You're being a pug.

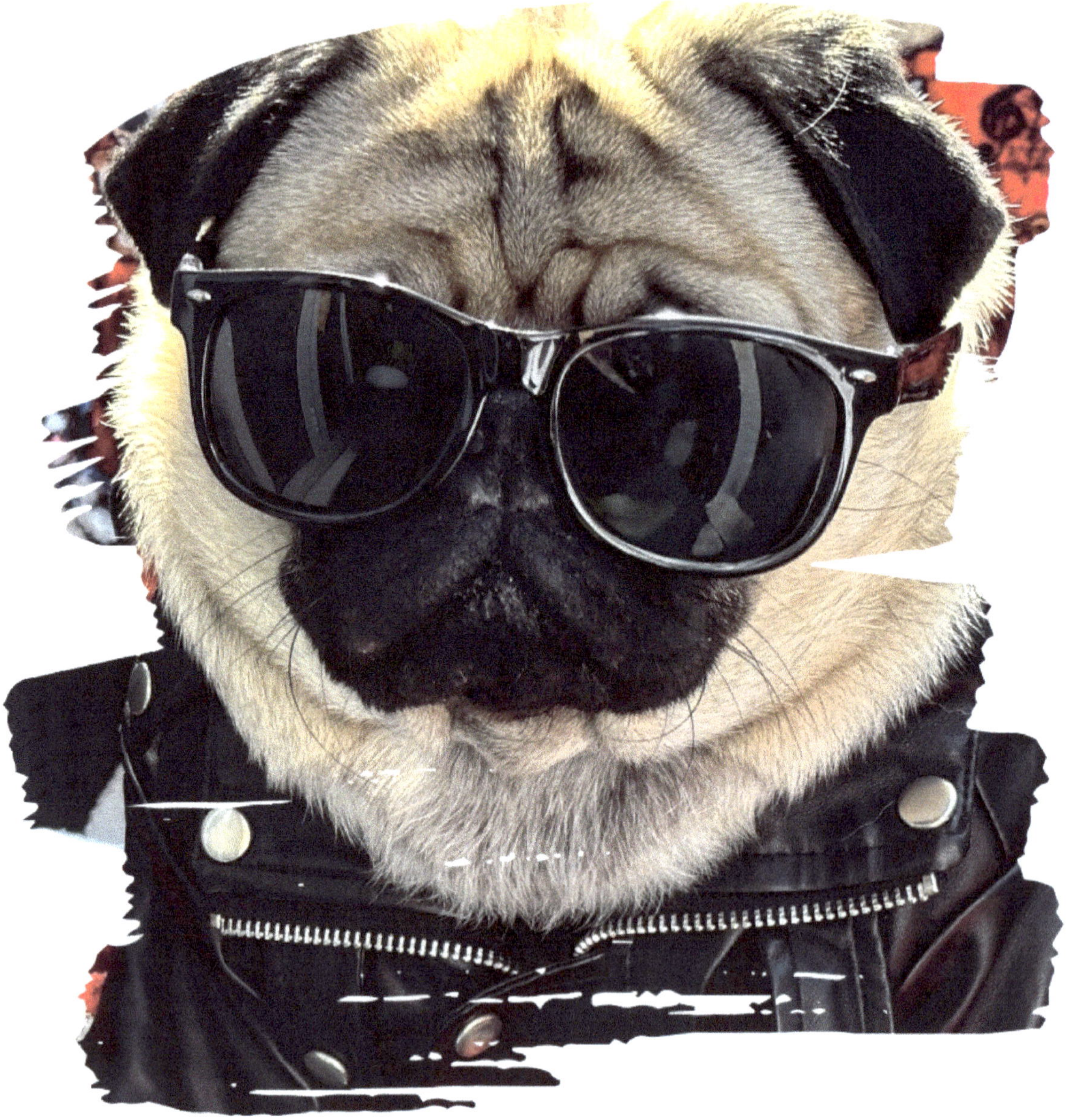

The Leather Jacket Days

Phil-osophical Quote:

"Some days you need a jacket that says, 'don't mess with me'—even if you cry in it later."

Phil's Emotional Outfit Notes:

I wear leather when I need boundaries. When I need to feel strong. When I need the world to know I'm not here for nonsense. It doesn't mean I'm not soft underneath. It means I'm protecting the softness. With zips.

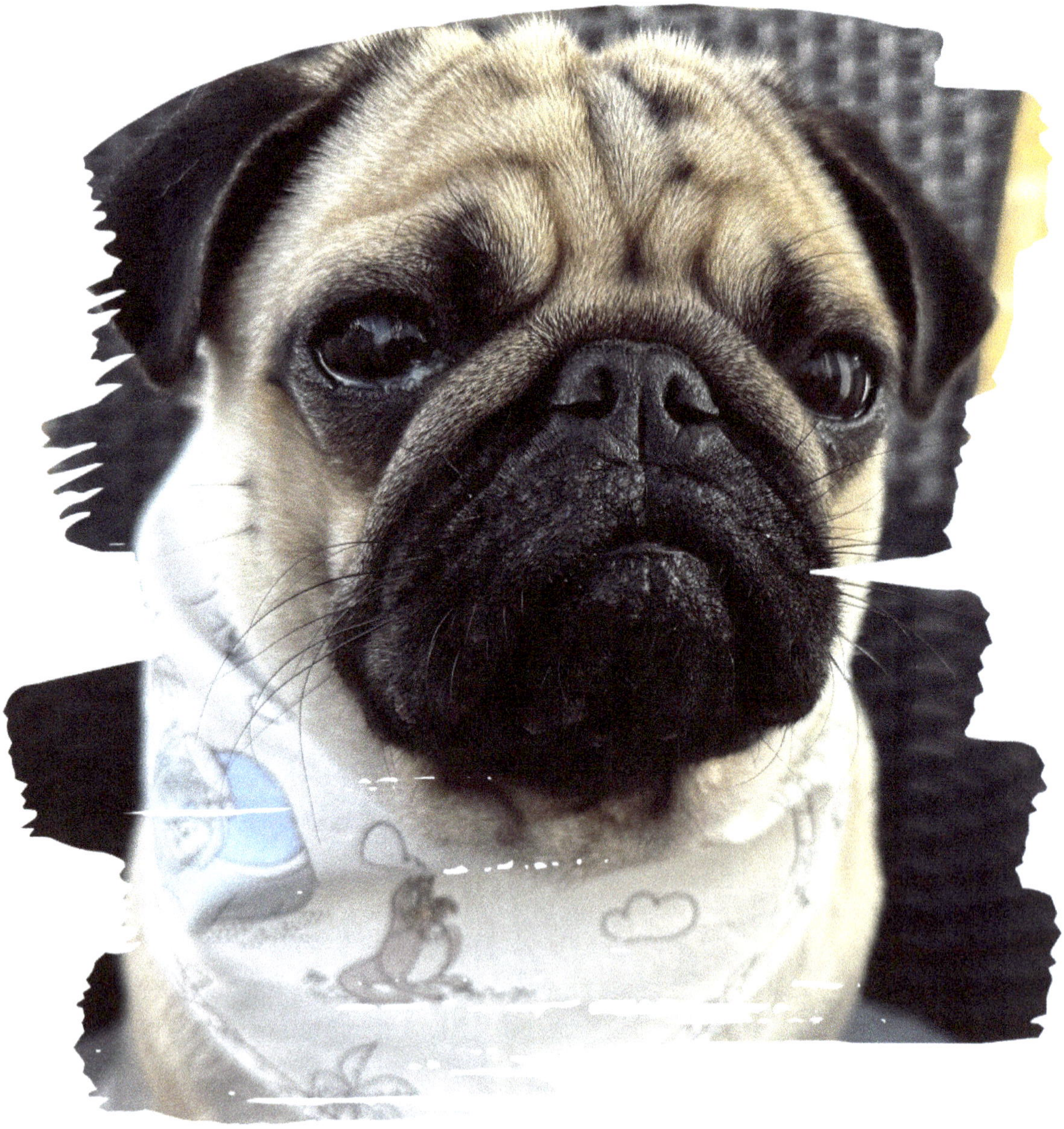

The Bandana of Bravery

Phil-osophical Quote:

"If the bandana makes you feel powerful... wear it to the meeting."

Phil's Emotional Outfit Notes:

I wear the bandana when I want to feel bold. When I want to walk into the room like I own the biscuit tin. When I want to remind myself that softness and swagger can coexist. It's not about the look. It's about the feeling. And the feeling is: confident, loved, and slightly snack obsessed.

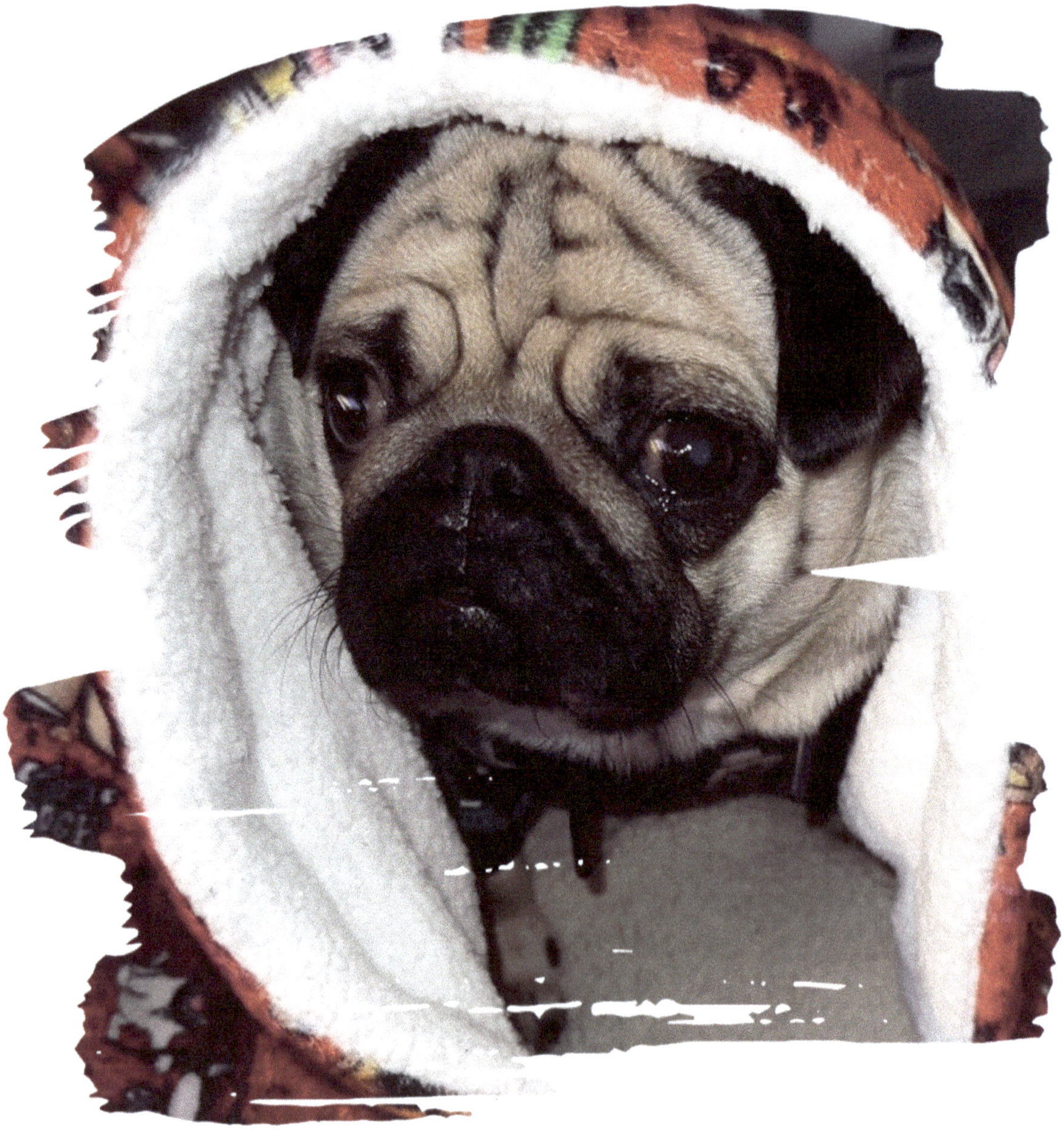

The Blanket Cape

Phil-osophical Quote:

"Sometimes the cape is just a blanket you refused to take off. That's okay."

Phil's Emotional Outfit Notes:

I wear the blanket when I need comfort. When I'm not ready to face the world. When I want to feel held. It becomes a cape when I decide I'm still powerful— even in my softness.

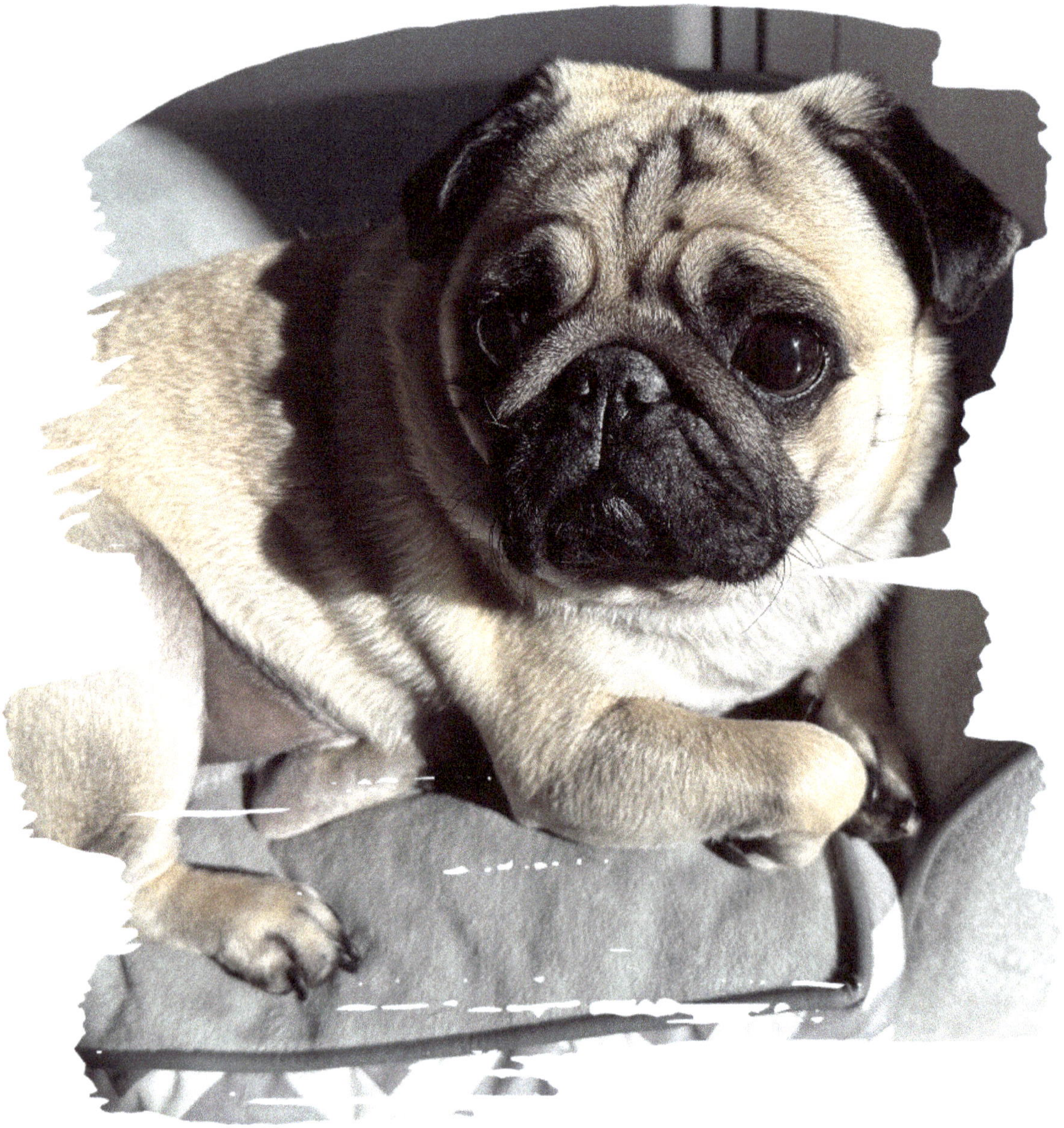

The Naked Confidence Look

Phil-osophical Quote:

"No outfit. Just vibes."

Phil's Emotional Outfit Notes:

Some days I wear nothing. No jacket. No bandana. Just me. That's enough.
Confidence isn't always loud. Sometimes it's a quiet snort and a bare belly in the
sunbeam.

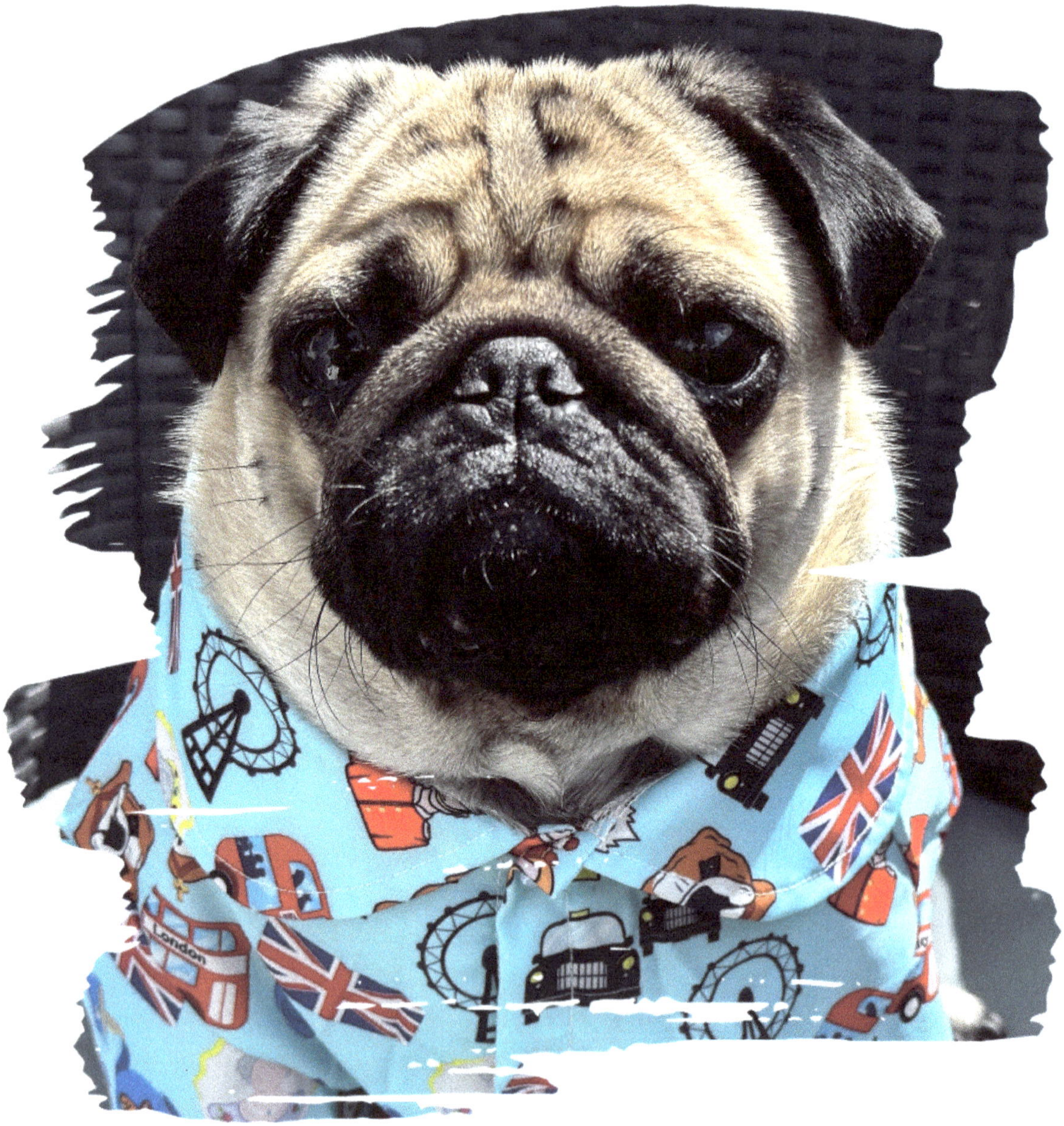
London

🧠 Phil's Final Pawse

Phil-osophical Quote:

"Dress how you feel. Or how you want to feel. Or just for the drama."

Phil's Emotional Outfit Notes:

Fashion is feelings. Feelings are valid. You are valid. Whether you're in leather, fluff, bold colours, or nothing at all—you're being a pug – you're being you.

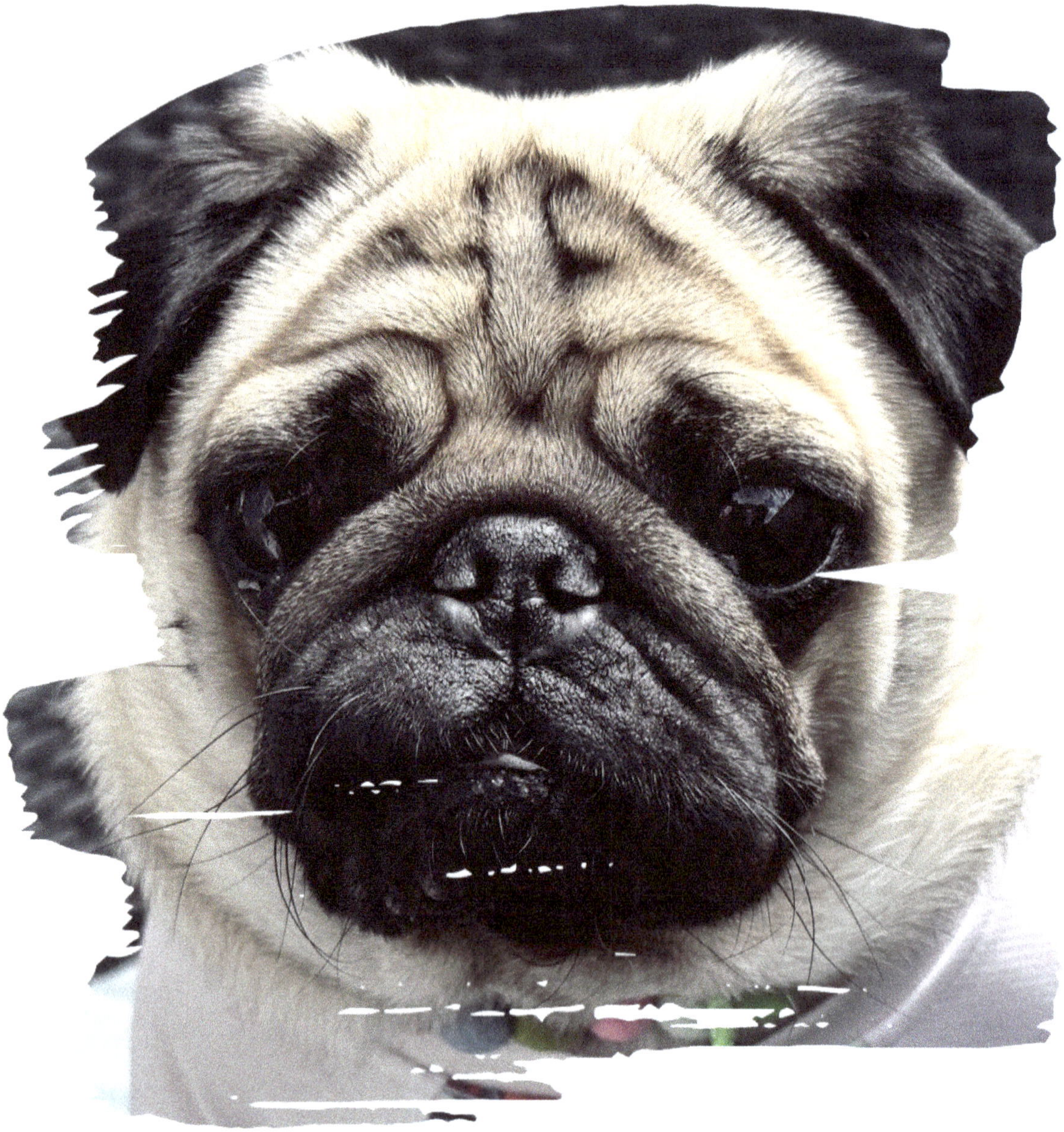

Chapter 5: Phil's Soft Thoughts & Quiet Courage

Because sometimes the quietest thought carries the loudest truth

Welcome to Chapter Five. Or as I call it: The Department of Emotional Snorts.

This is where we talk about feelings. The big ones. The small ones. The ones you don't know how to name yet.

I'm not a therapist. I'm a pug. But I've felt things. I've watched the rain from the window and wondered if I'm still snack-worthy, or will the park still be there once the rain stops. I've curled up in a blanket and remembered that I am and it will be.

This chapter is about emotional literacy, quiet courage, and the kind of softness that makes you strong. You're allowed to feel it all. You're being a pug, – and being true to you.

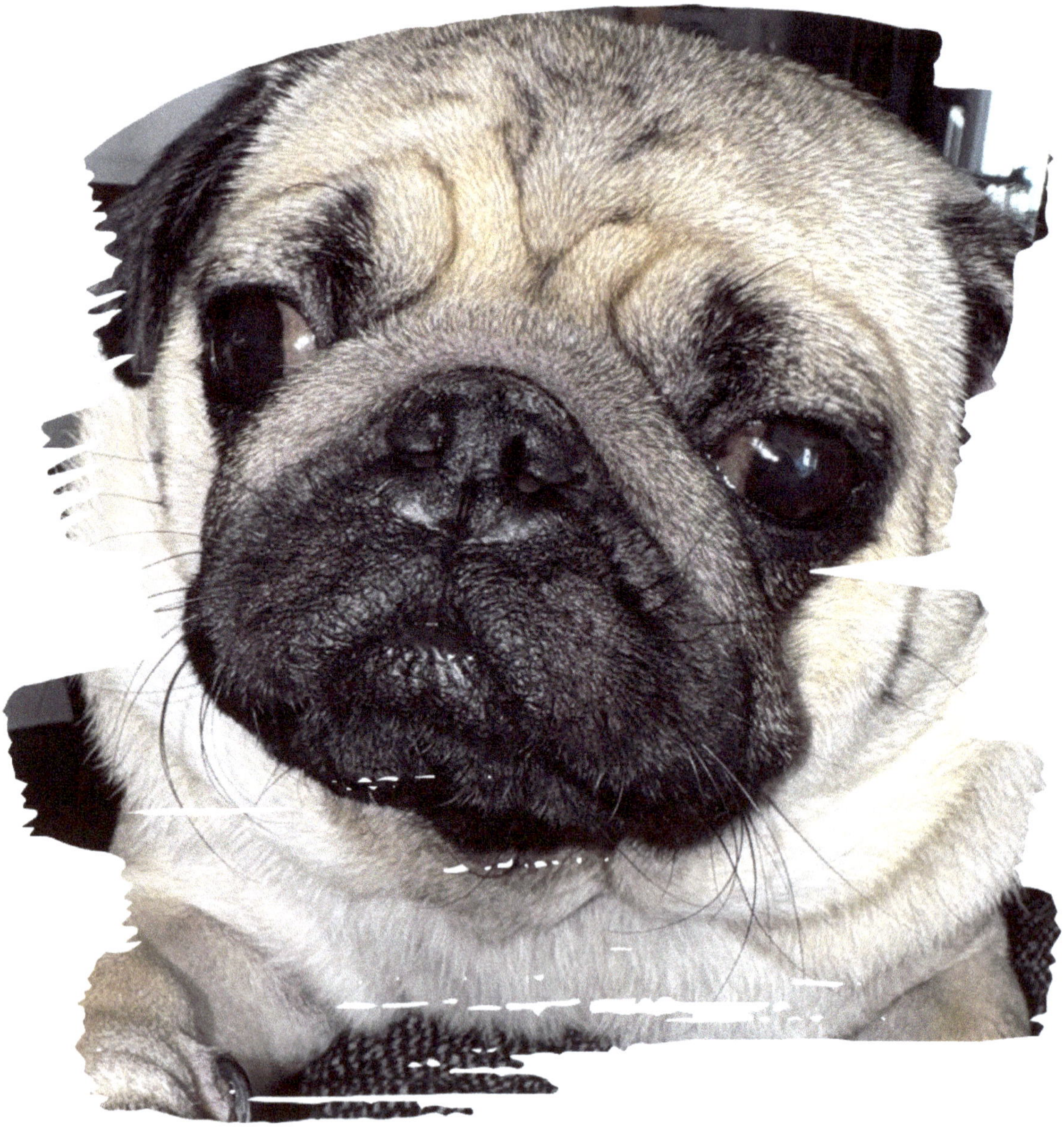

The Quiet Snort of Sadness

Phil-osophical Quote:

"Sad is not a failure. It's just a feeling."

Phil's Soul Snort:

Sometimes I snort quietly. Not because I'm tired. But because I'm sad. And that's okay. Sadness isn't weakness. It's honesty. It's your heart saying, "I need a moment." Take the moment. Take the break. You're allowed.

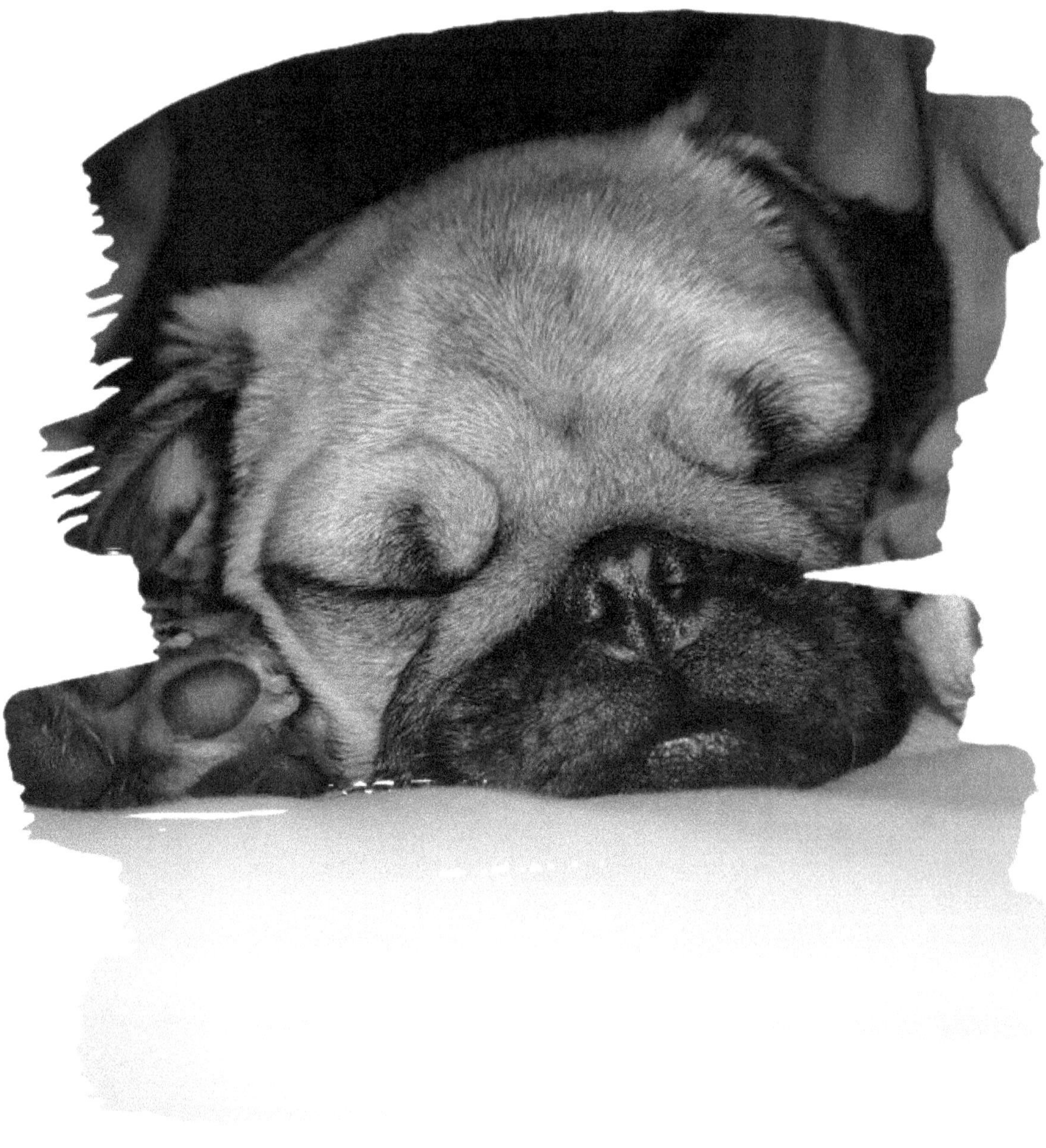

The Big Feeling Nap

Phil-osophical Quote:

"Feel it. Nap it. Heal it."

Phil's Soul Snort:

Big feelings are exhausting. Sometimes the best thing you can do is nap. Not to escape. But to rest. To reset. To remind yourself that healing doesn't have to be loud. You're allowed to pause. You're allowed to snore through the storm.

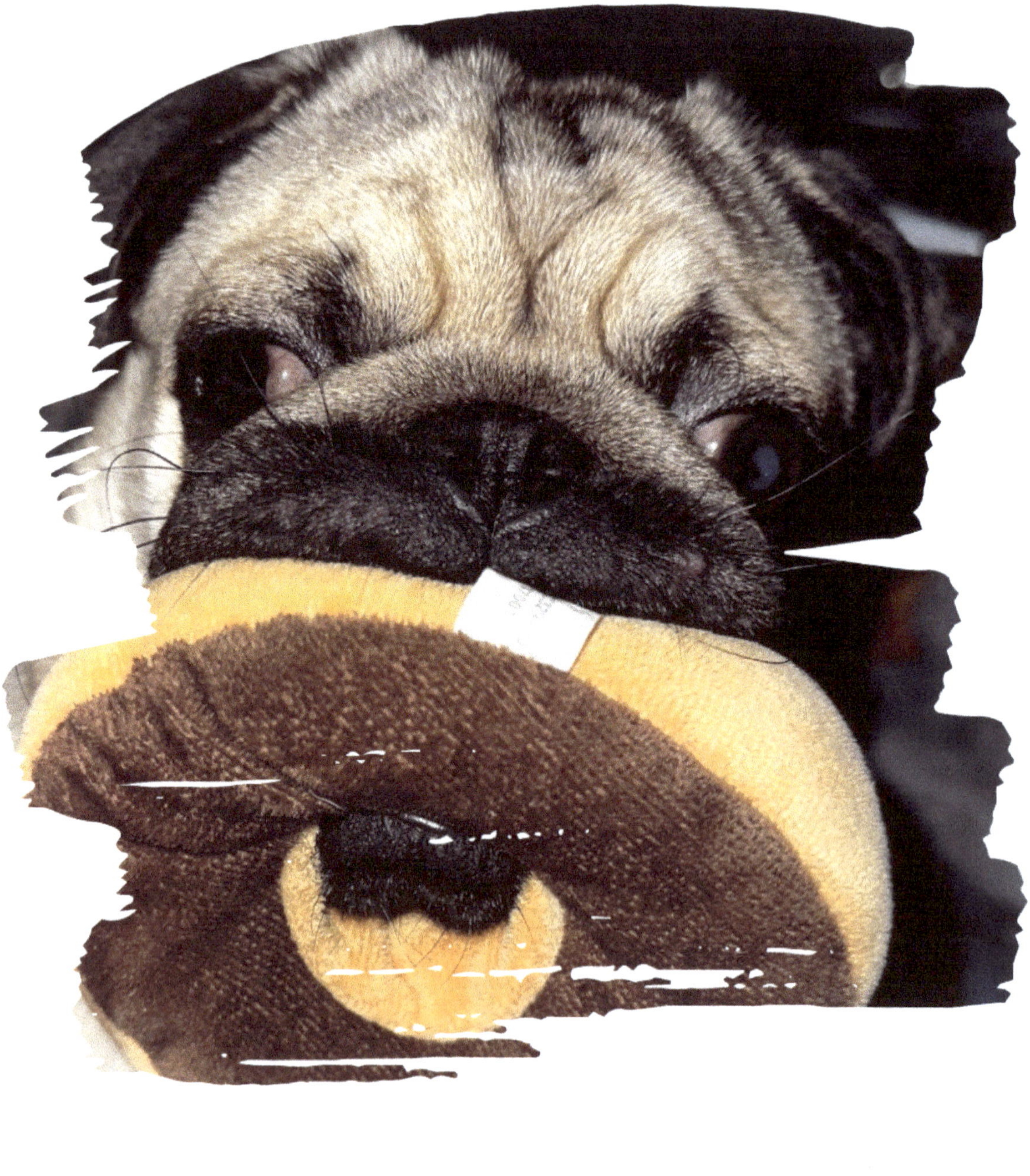

The Joy Object

Phil-osophical Quote:

"Sometimes the squeaky toy is emotional support. Sometimes it's just joy."

Phil's Soul Snort:

I don't always know what I need. But sometimes, it's my favourite toy. Not because I'm bored. But because it makes me feel like myself again. Like I'm allowed to play, even when the world feels heavy.

Your version might be painting. Or running. Or rearranging your sock drawer. Whatever brings you back to you—that's your joy object. That's emotional support.

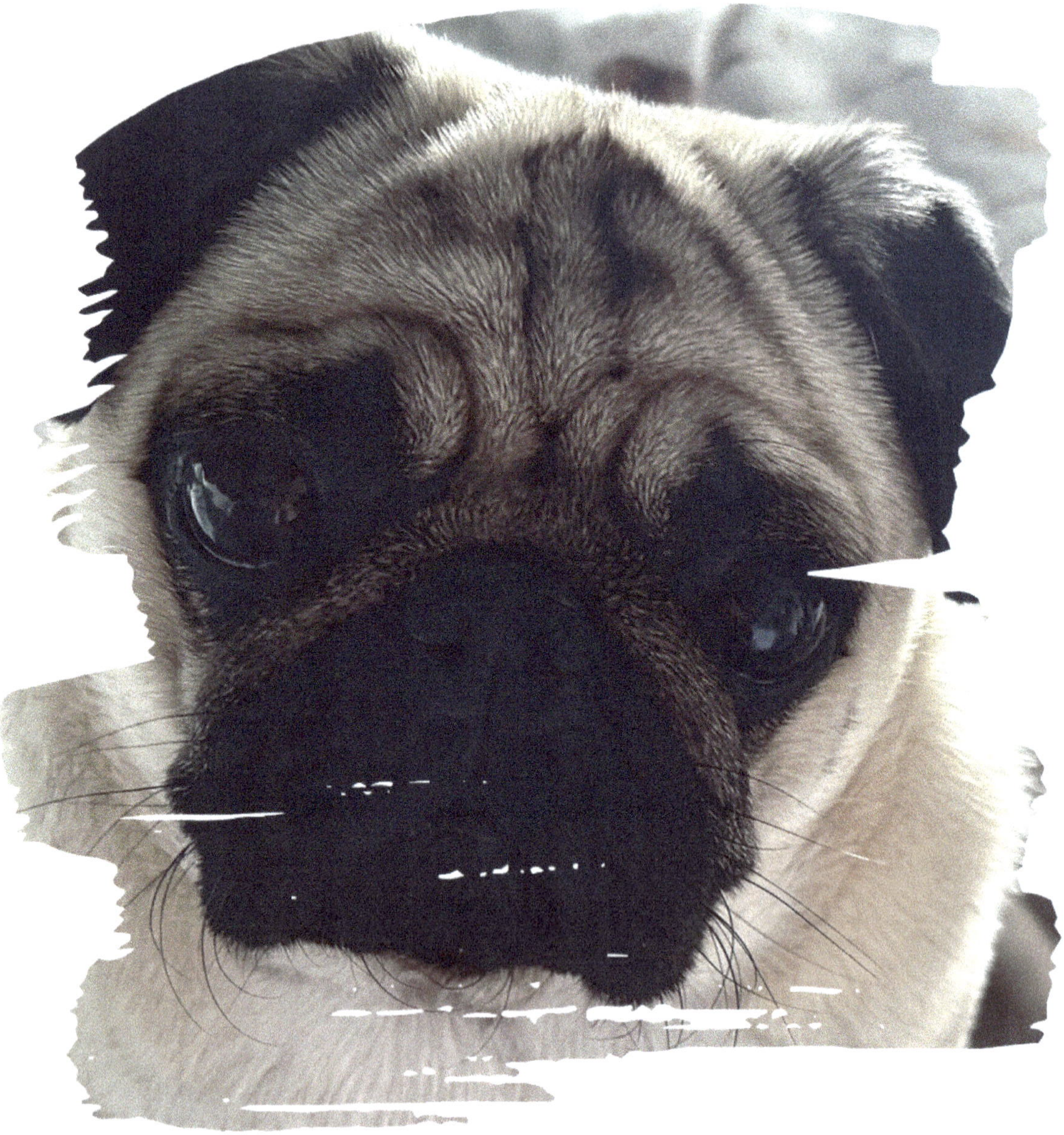

The Snort of Self-Compassion

Phil-osophical Quote:

"Talk to yourself like you would to me."

Phil's Take:

You'd never tell me I'm too much. You'd never rush me through a bad day. You'd never take away my biscuit when I'm sad. So don't do it to yourself. Be gentle. Be kind. Be the voice you'd use with a pug in a puddle.

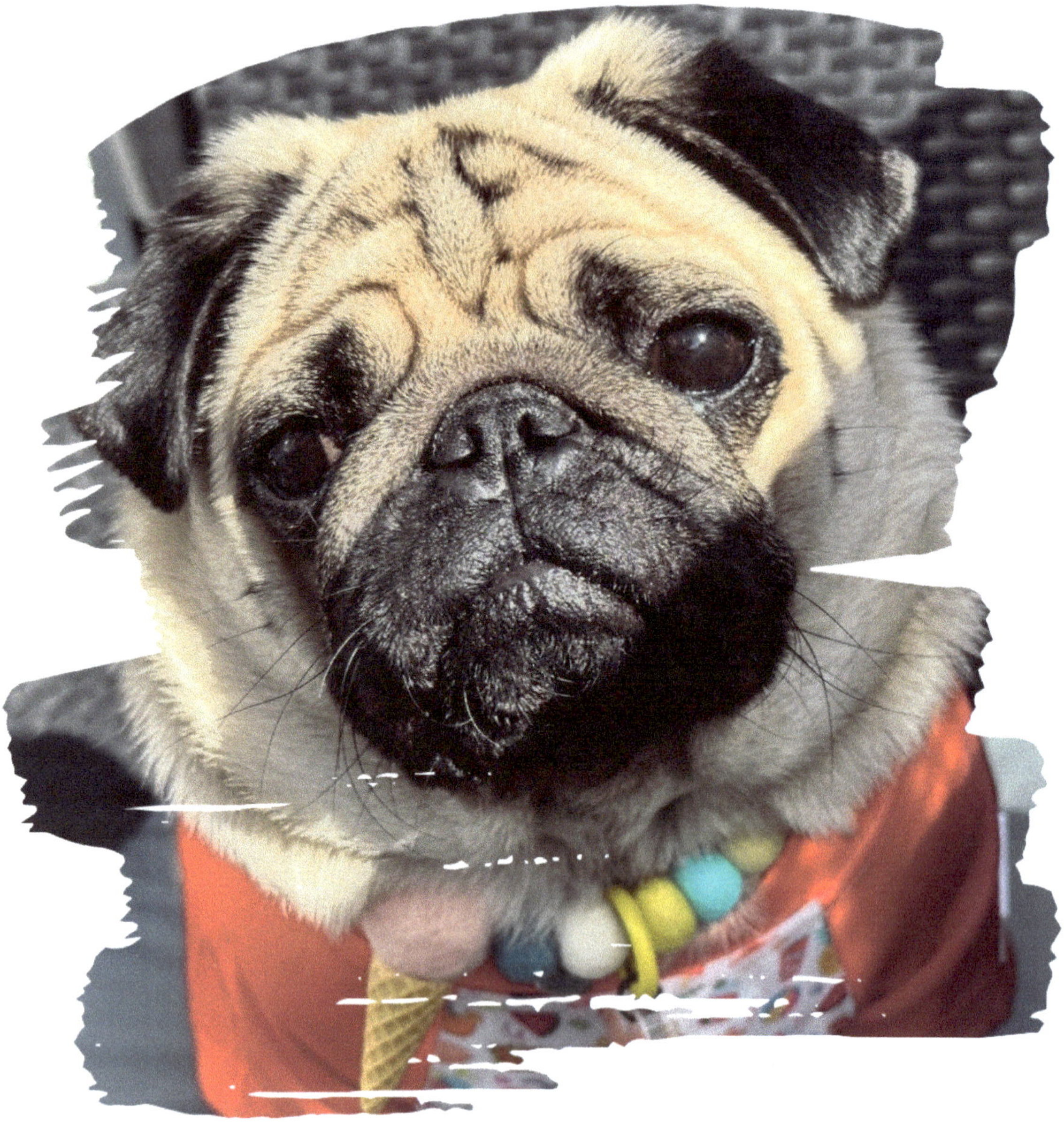

🧠 Phil's Final Pawse

Phil-osophical Quote:

"Soft is strong. Sad is valid. You are loved."

Phil's Soul Snort:

You don't have to be cheerful all the time. You don't have to be brave every minute. You just have to be real. And real includes softness, sadness, and snorts. You're being a pug. And that's more than enough.

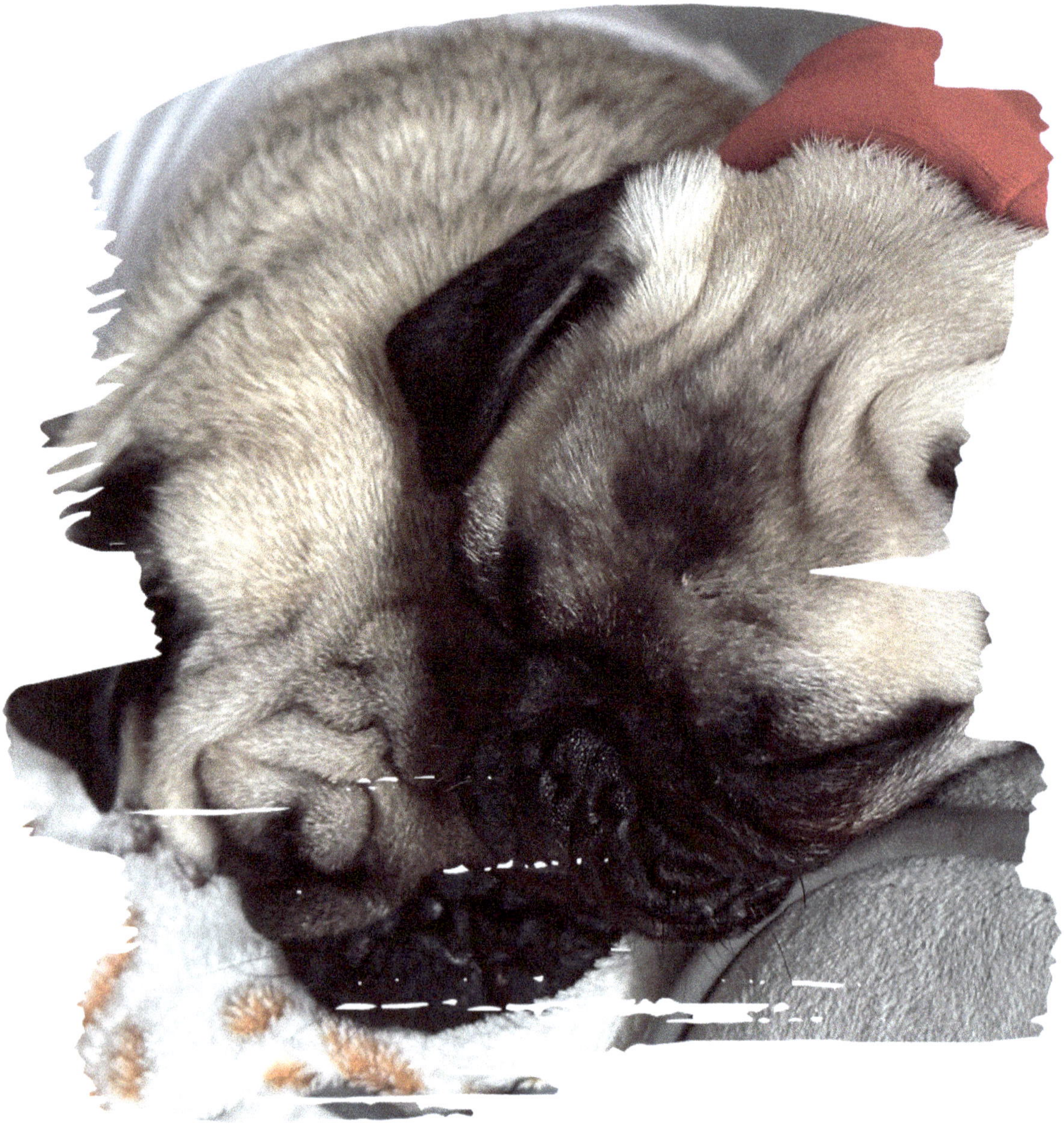

Chapter 6: How to Share Your Blanket (and Your Heart)

Because emotional generosity should never leave you cold

Welcome to Chapter Six. The chapter where we talk about sharing—not just snacks, but space, energy, and emotional fluff.

Sharing your blanket is a metaphor. It means letting someone in. It means trusting them with your softness. But here's the thing: not everyone deserves your blanket. Some people just want the warmth without the weight.

This chapter is about emotional generosity—with boundaries. It's about knowing when to snort, when to scoot over, and when to walk away with your blanket still wrapped around you.

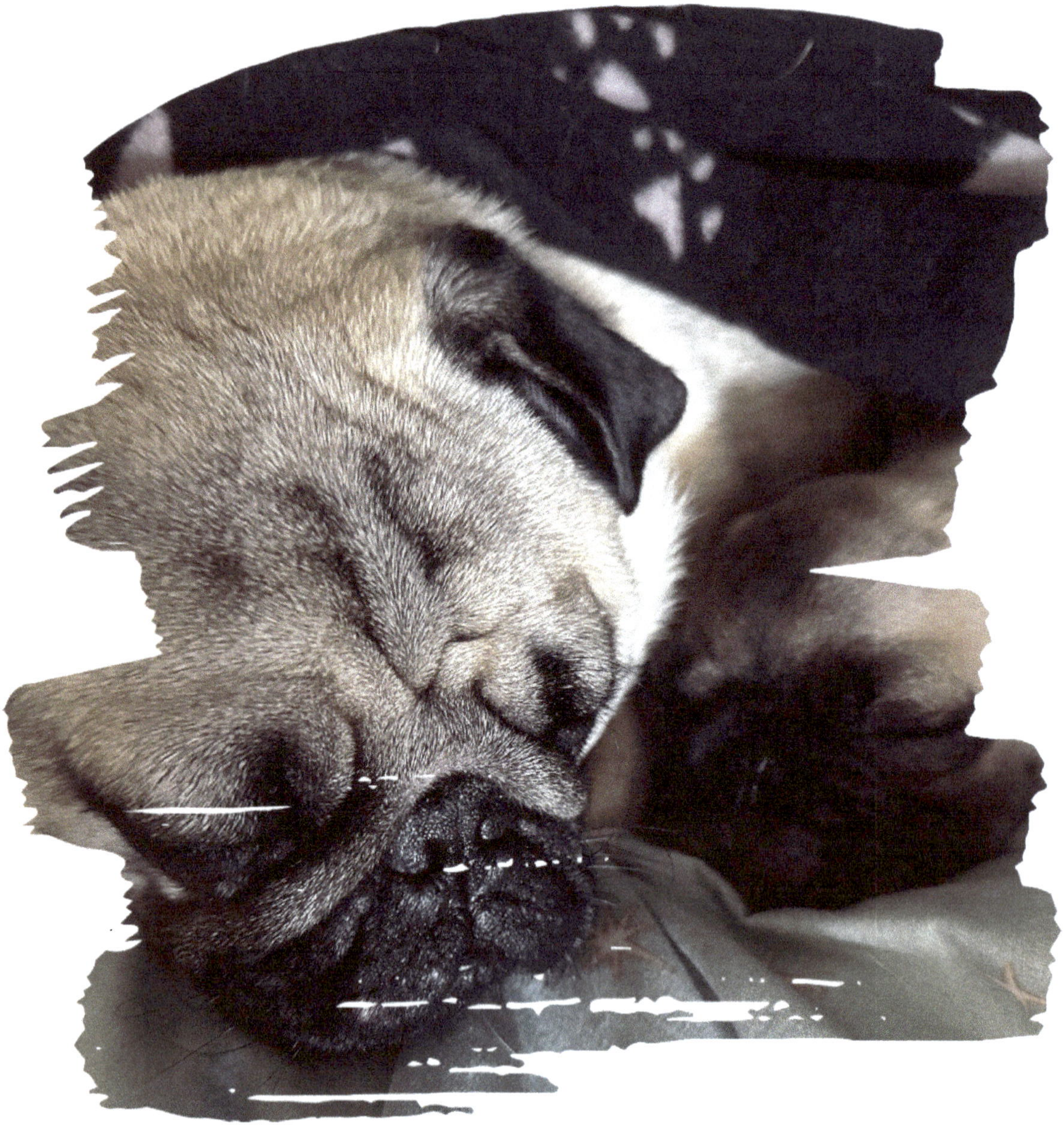

The Blanket Test

Phil-osophical Quote:

"If they steal the blanket and don't share the snuggles... reconsider."

Phil's Inner Snort:

I've shared my blanket with plushies, hoomans, one very entitled cat, and my brother George. Some gave snuggles back (George). Some just took the warmth (cat). You deserve reciprocity. If they're not bringing comfort, maybe they don't belong under your blanket.

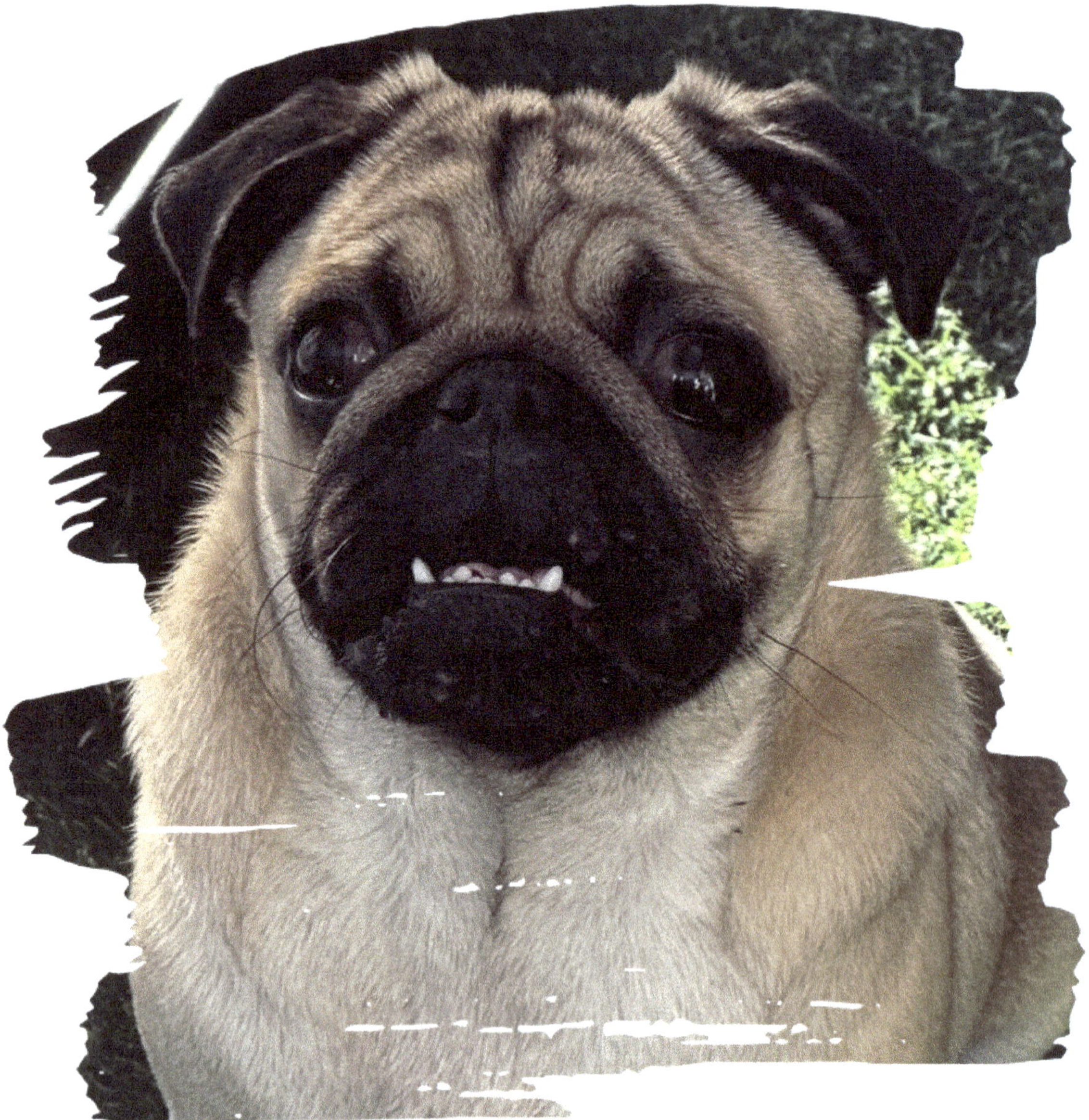

The Shared Snort Agreement

Phil-osophical Quote:

"If they laugh at your snort, not with it... that's not sharing."

Phil's Inner Snort:

My snort is part of me. It's loud. It's weird. It's wonderful. Sharing yourself means being seen and celebrated—not mocked. Find the ones who snort with you. They're your hoomans.

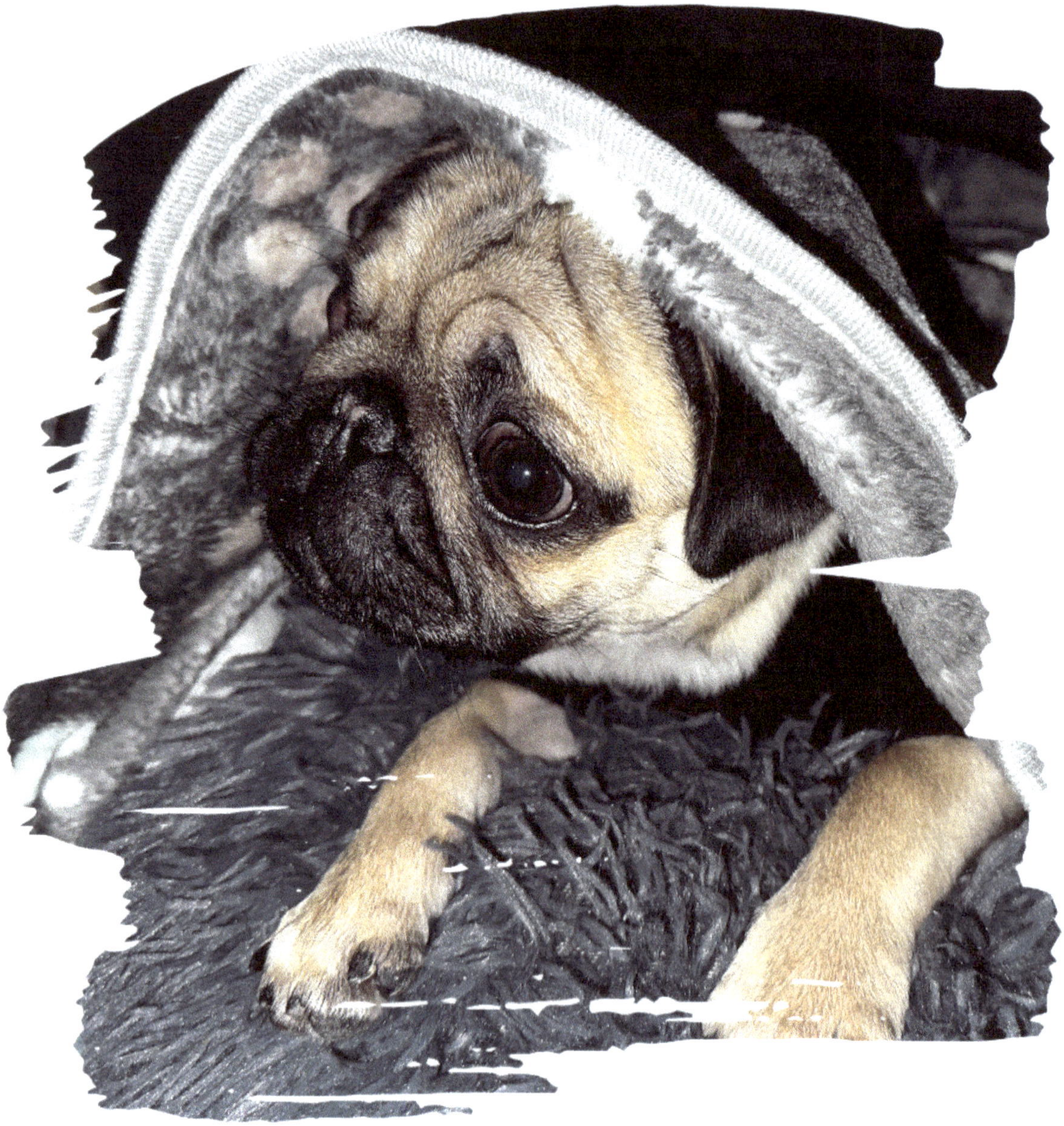

The Blanket Reclaim

Phil-osophical Quote:

"Taking your blanket back isn't rude. It's self-respect."

Phil's Inner Snort:

Sometimes I give too much. Too many snuggles. Too much warmth. But I've learned to reclaim my blanket. To wrap myself up again. To say, "I need this more than you do right now." That's not selfish. That's self-care.

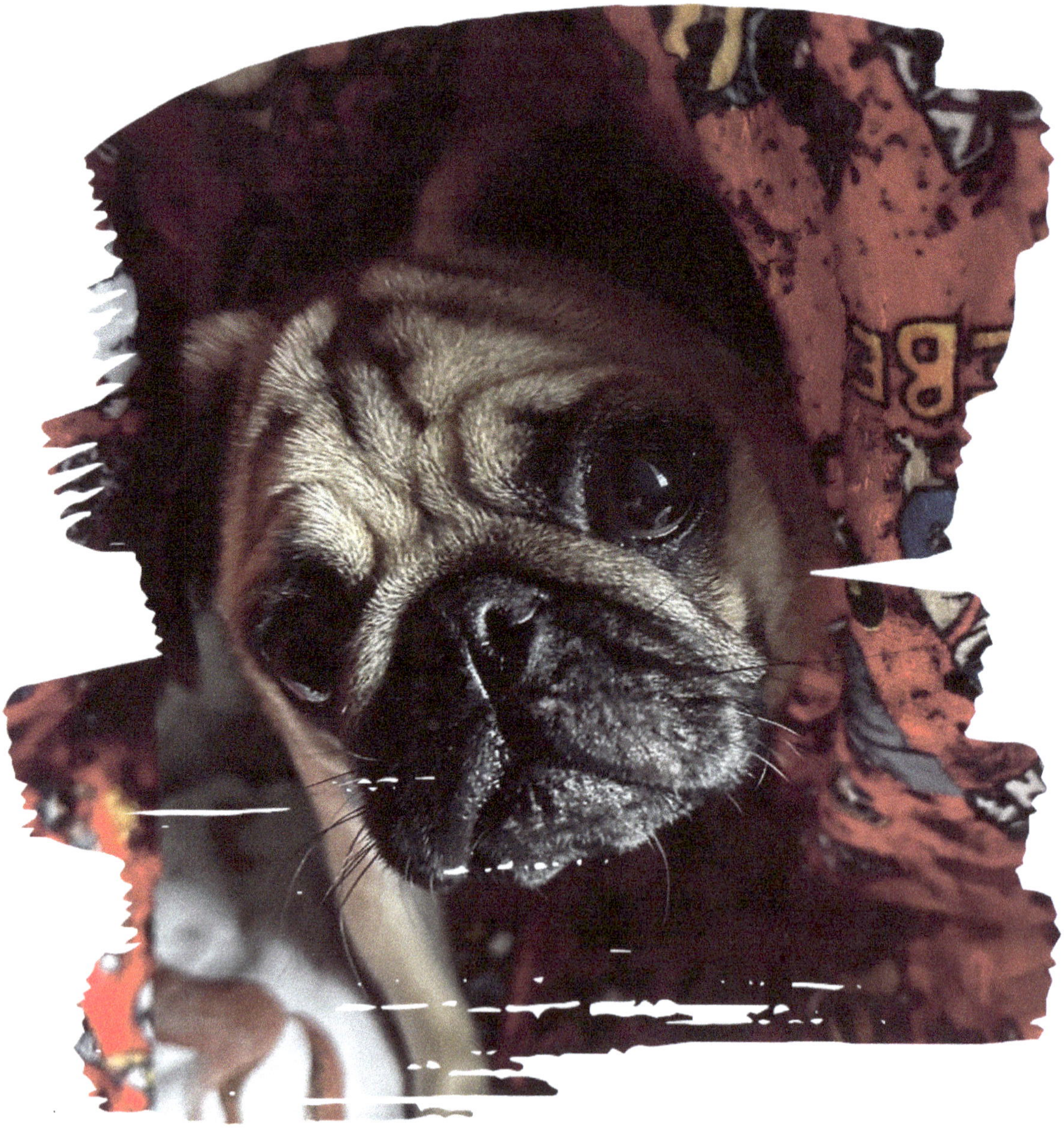

🧠 Phil's Final Pawse

Phil-osophical Quote:

"You can share your heart. Just don't give it away without a snort clause."

Phil's Inner Snort:

Sharing is beautiful. But boundaries are what make it safe. You're allowed to be generous. You're also allowed to be discerning. Wrap your blanket around those who earn it. And keep a corner for yourself.

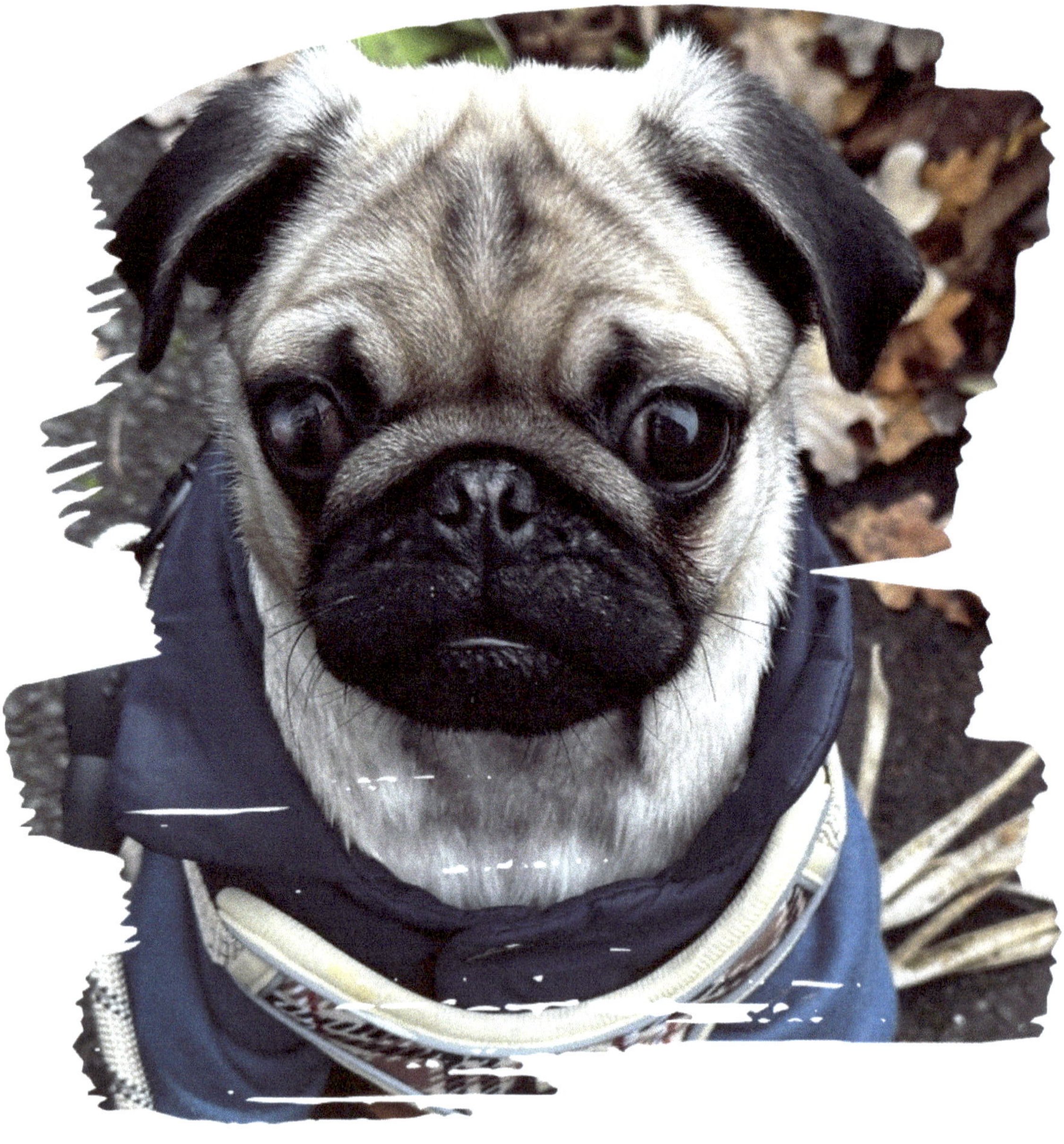

🐾 Chapter 7: Friendship & Emotional Fences

Because not every tail wag means forever

Welcome to Chapter Seven. The one where we talk about friendship, loyalty, and the emotional chaos of the dog park.

I've been ghosted by a cockapoo. Followed and unfollowed by a schnauzer. Befriended by a labradoodle who only wanted my yak chew.

Friendship is weird. It's wonderful. It's sometimes disappointing. But it's also where the good stuff lives—like shared sniffs, mutual tail wags, and the kind of loyalty that doesn't flinch when you snort in public.

This chapter is for the ones who've felt left out, overlooked, or unfollowed. You're not alone. I get it. And I've got you.

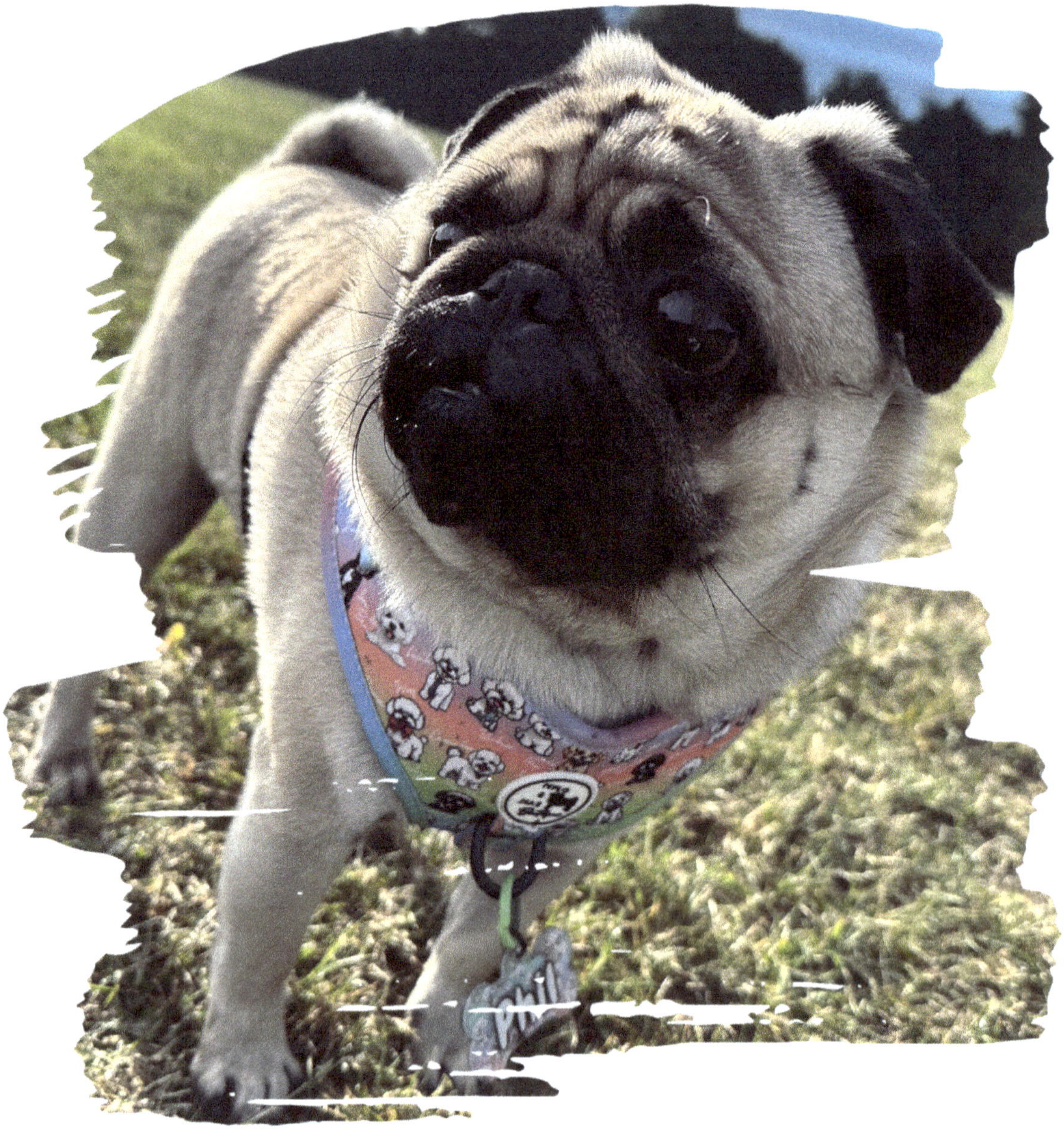

The Park Ghosting Incident

Phil-osophical Quote:

"One day they sniff you. The next day they pretend they've never smelled you."

From Phil's Heart:

I met a dog named Ruby. We sniffed. We played. We shared a moment. Next day?
Nothing. Not even a tail flick. It hurt. But I learned: not every sniff is a soul
contract. Some are just passing breezes. You're still worthy. Even when they walk
away.

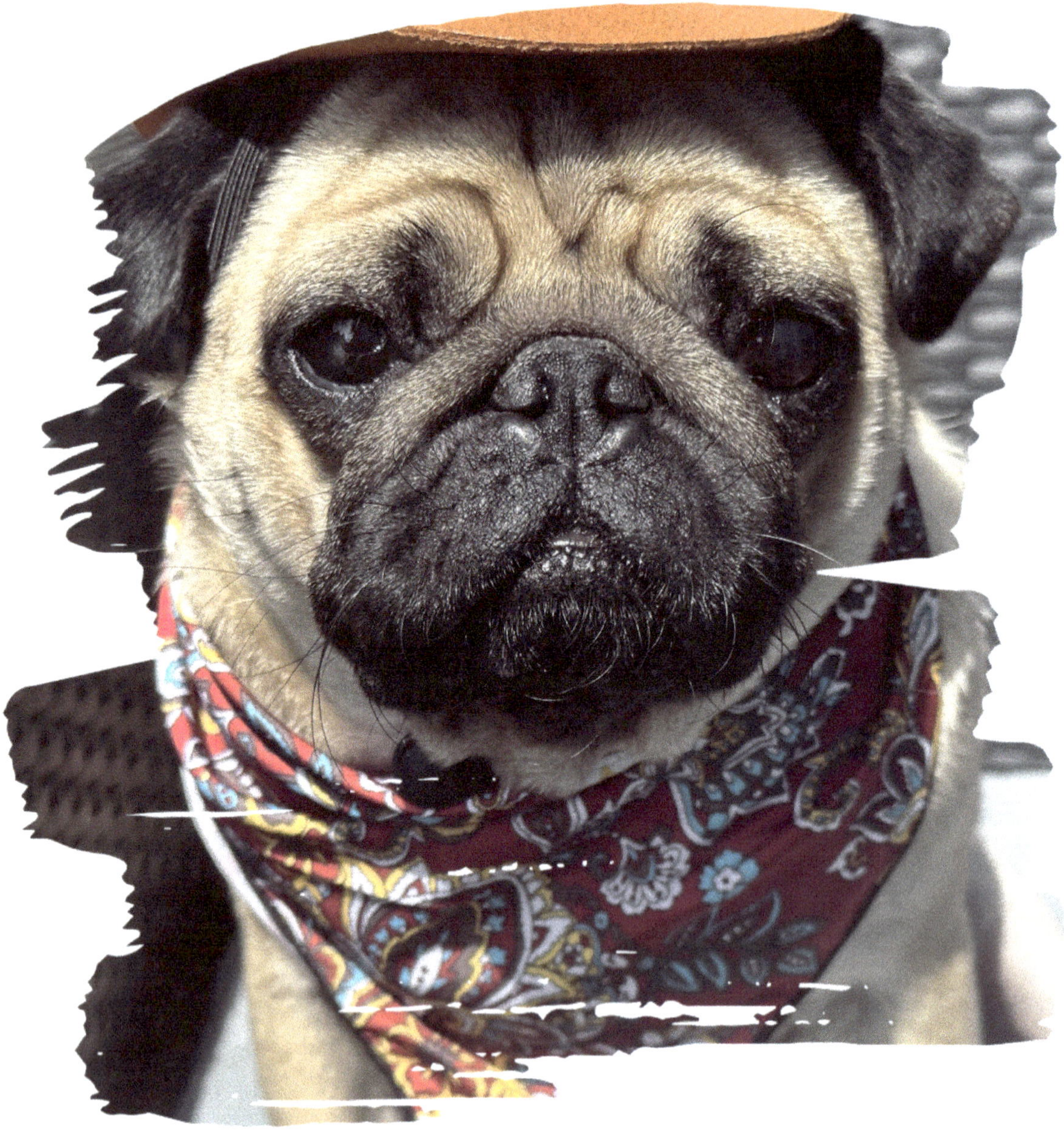

The Follow-Unfollow Phil-osophy

Phil-osophical Quote:

"If they unfollow, let them. Your snorts aren't for everyone."

From Phil's Heart:

I've got followers in Tokyo, Toronto, and Tunbridge Wells. Some stay. Some go. Some come back when I post a reel in a hat. Friendship isn't about numbers. It's about connection. And if they unfollow, let them. You're still fabulous.

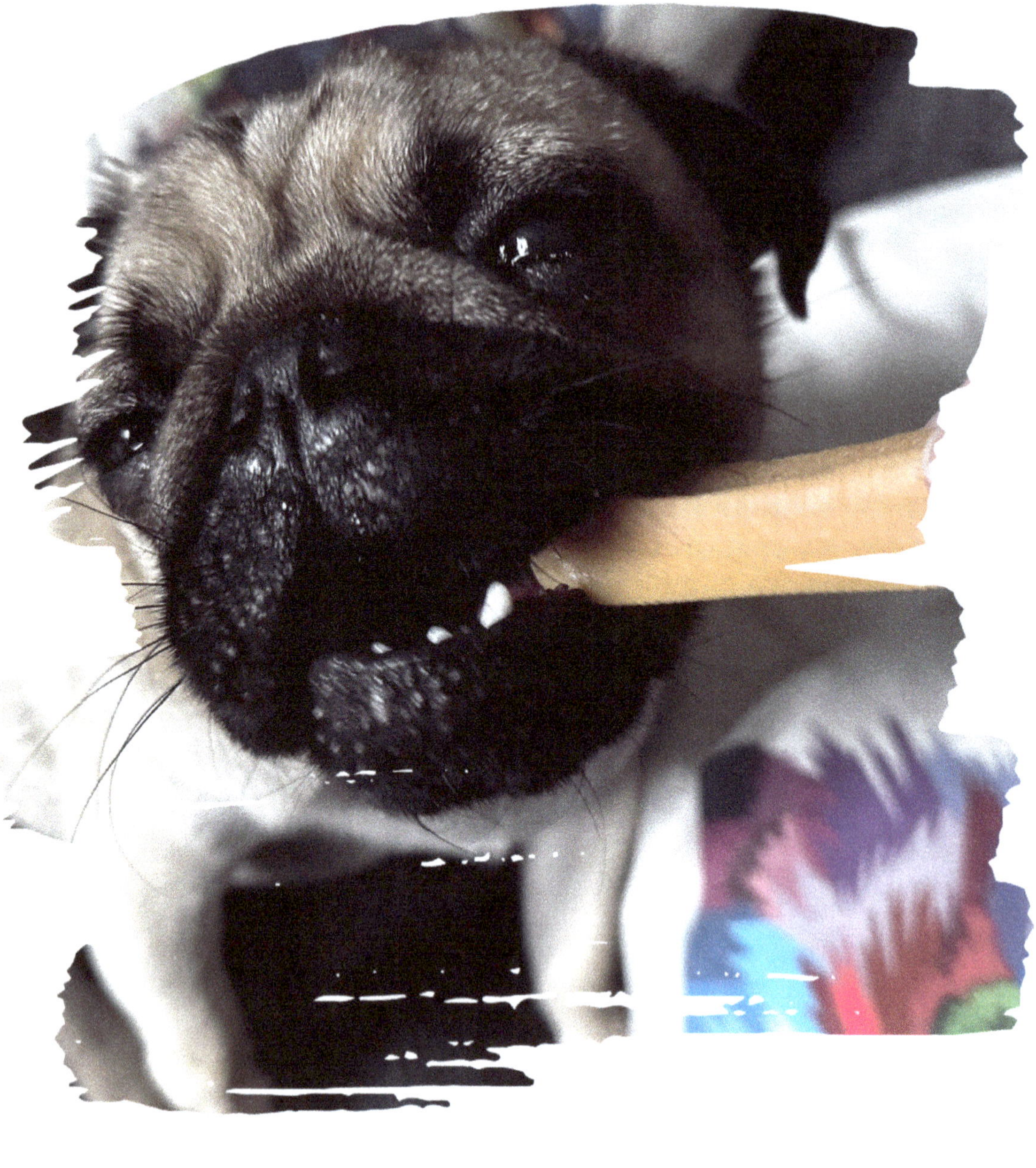

The Yak Chew Betrayal

Phil-osophical Quote:

"If they only want your yak... they're not your pack."

From Phil's Heart:

I once shared my yak chew with a spaniel named Luna. She took it. She ran. She never looked back. It taught me: generosity is beautiful. But protect your joy objects. Real friends don't just take—they stay.

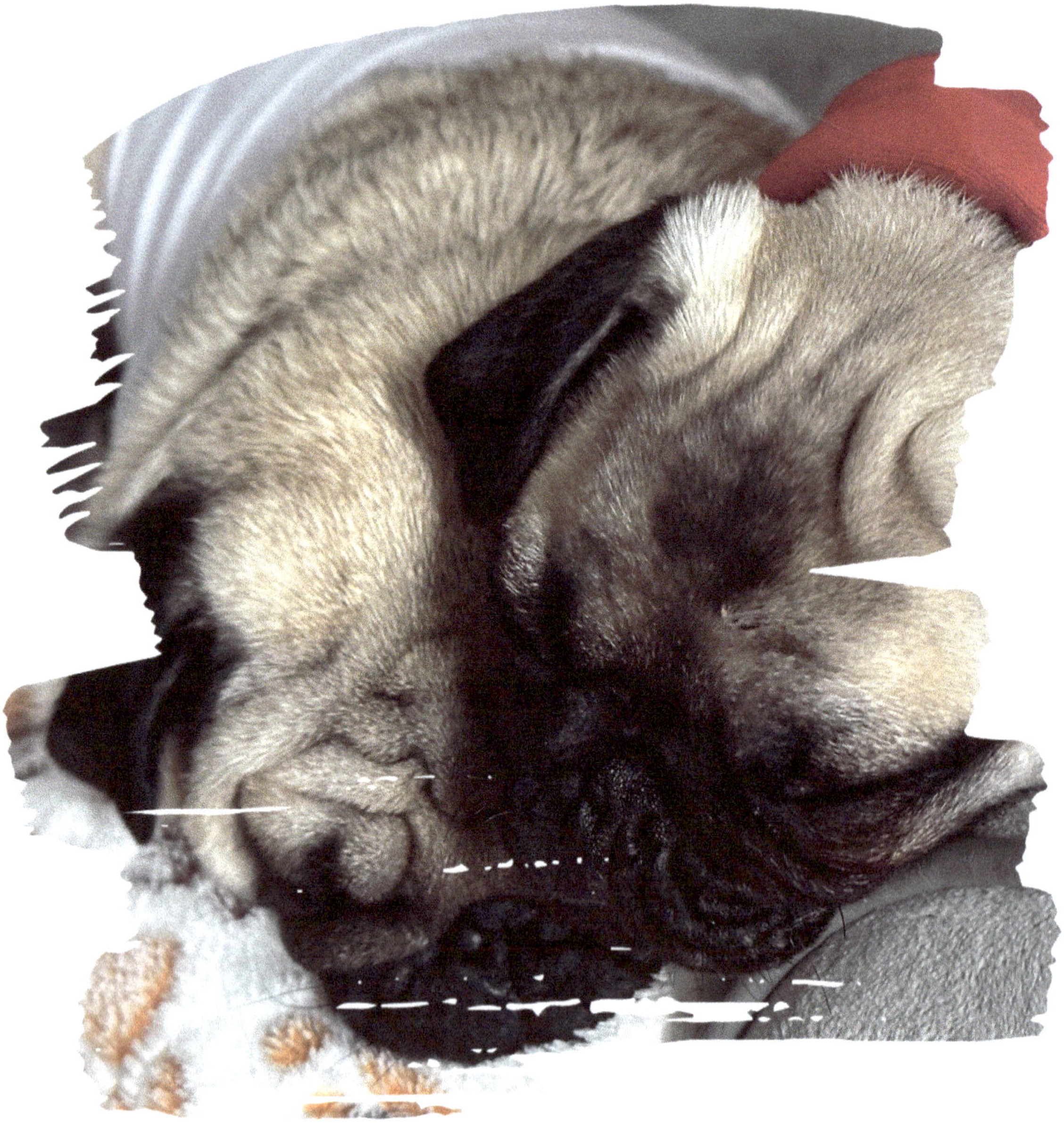

The Loyalty Test

Phil-osophical Quote:

"Loyalty isn't loud. It's who shows up when the snorts get messy."

From Phil's Heart:

I've had friends who stayed when I snorted through a thunderstorm. Who didn't flinch when I cried over a dropped sausage. That's loyalty. It's quiet. It's consistent. It's the kind of love that doesn't need a leash. Find those friends. Be that friend.

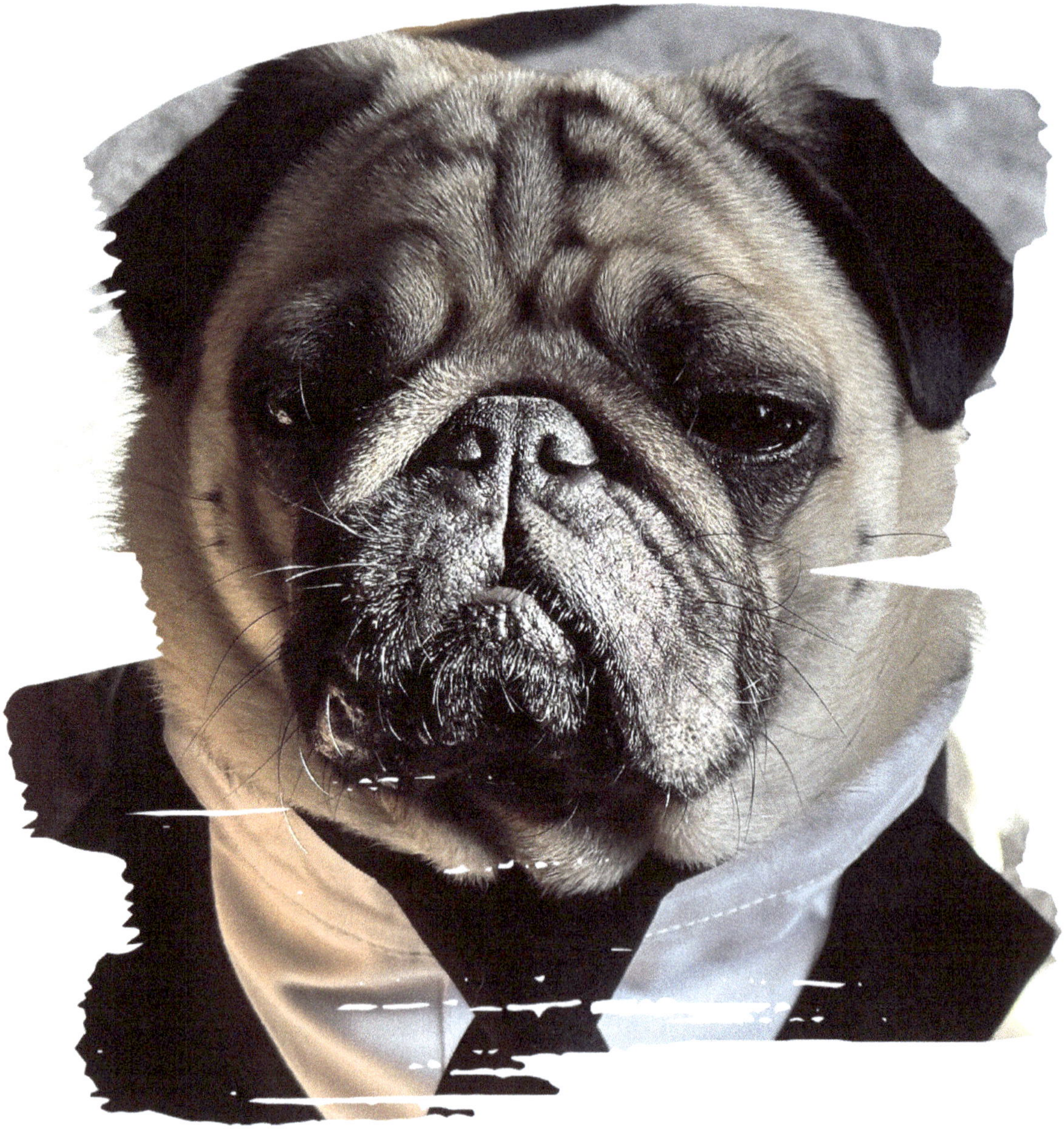

🧠 Phil's Friendship Manifesto

Phil-osophical Quote:

"You're not too much. You're just not for everyone. And that's okay."

From Phil's Heart:

You're allowed to be quirky. Loud. Soft. Selective. You're allowed to unfollow people who drain your tail wag. You're allowed to walk away from the park politics. You're allowed to be fully you—and still be loved. I see you. I follow you. I don't unfollow. Ever.

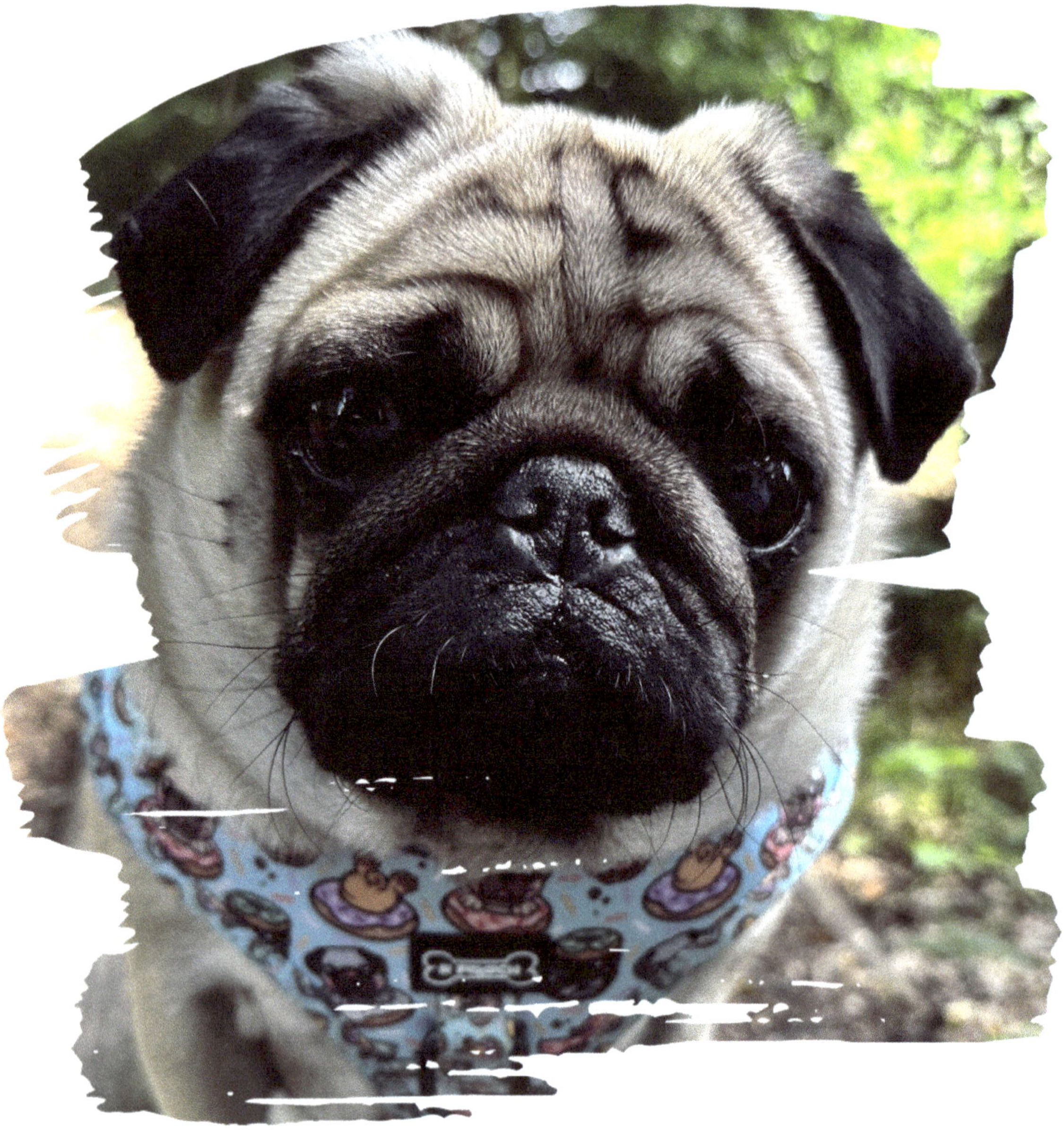

Chapter 8: Phil's Guide to Good Hoomans

Because some tail wags are earned. And some aren't

Welcome to Chapter Eight. The one where we talk about hoomans.

I've met the kind ones. The ones who sit with me when I'm quiet. Who wait for me to come to them. Who never rush the sniff.

I've also met the others. The ones who pull too hard. Who laugh when I flinch. Who forget that softness is sacred.

This chapter is about choosing wisely. About trusting your tail. About spotting the ones who see you—not just your cuteness, but your soul.

It's for dogs. It's for humans. It's for anyone who's ever been hurt and still wants to believe in kindness.

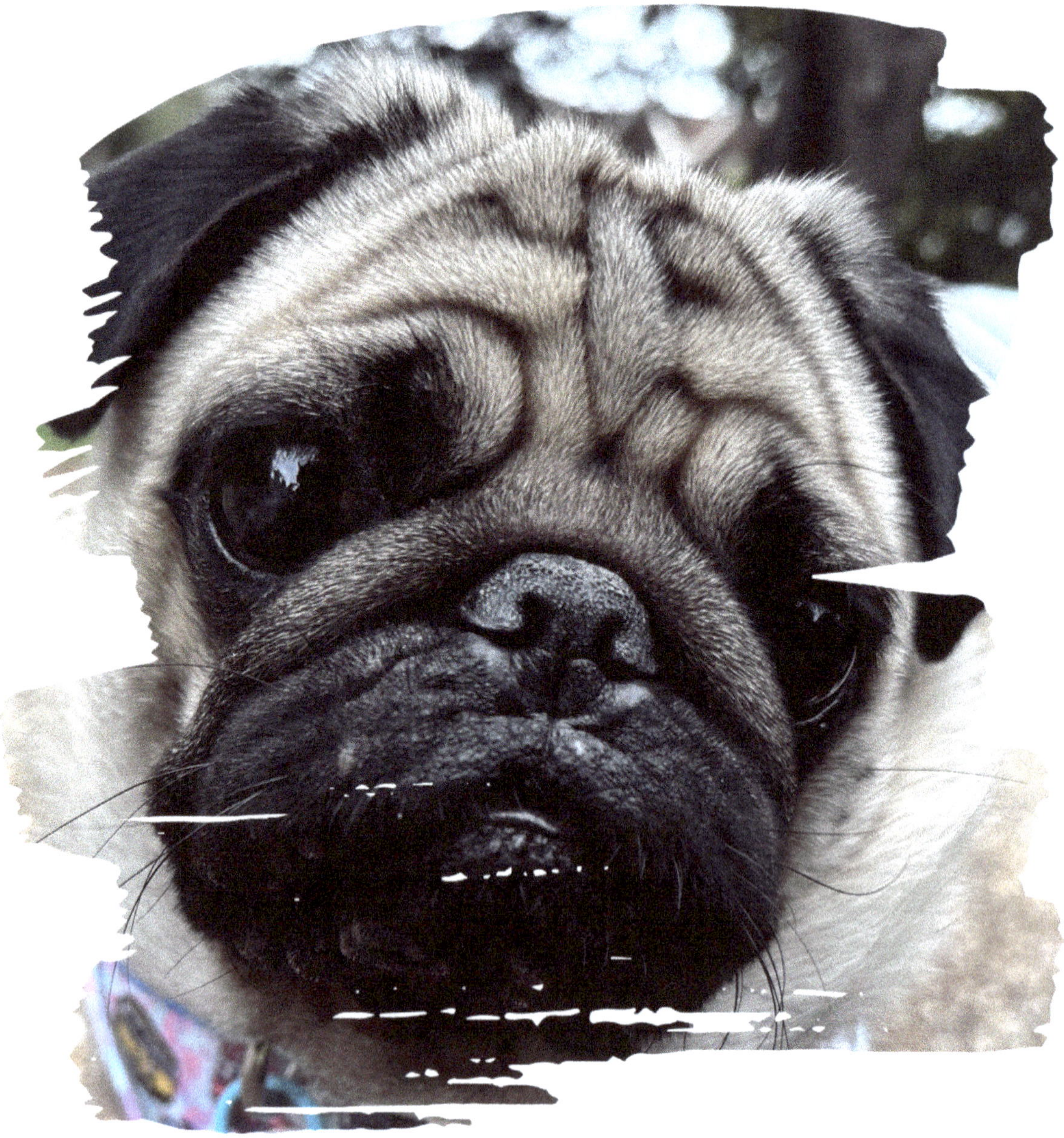

The Gentle Reach

Phil-osophical Quote:

"If they reach slowly, they've probably been hurt too."

From Phil's Heart:

Fast hands scare me. Loud voices make me shrink. But the gentle ones? They move like they understand. They've felt fear. They've earned trust. They're safe.

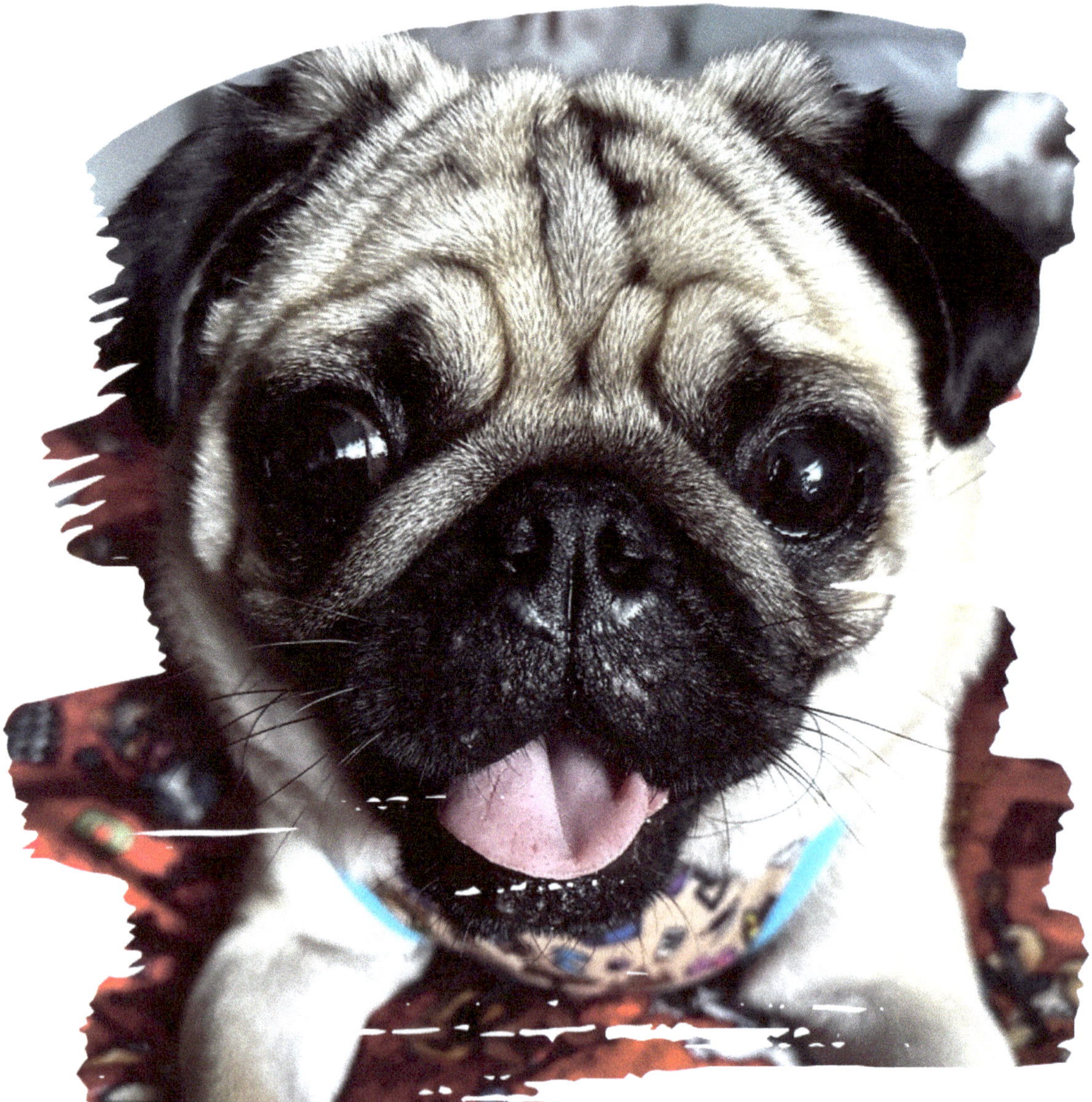

The Tail-Wag Echo

Phil-osophical Quote:

"If your tail wags and theirs does too... keep them."

From Phil's Heart:

Joy is contagious. But only with the right people. The good hoomans mirror your happiness. They celebrate your weirdness. They wag back. That's how you know.

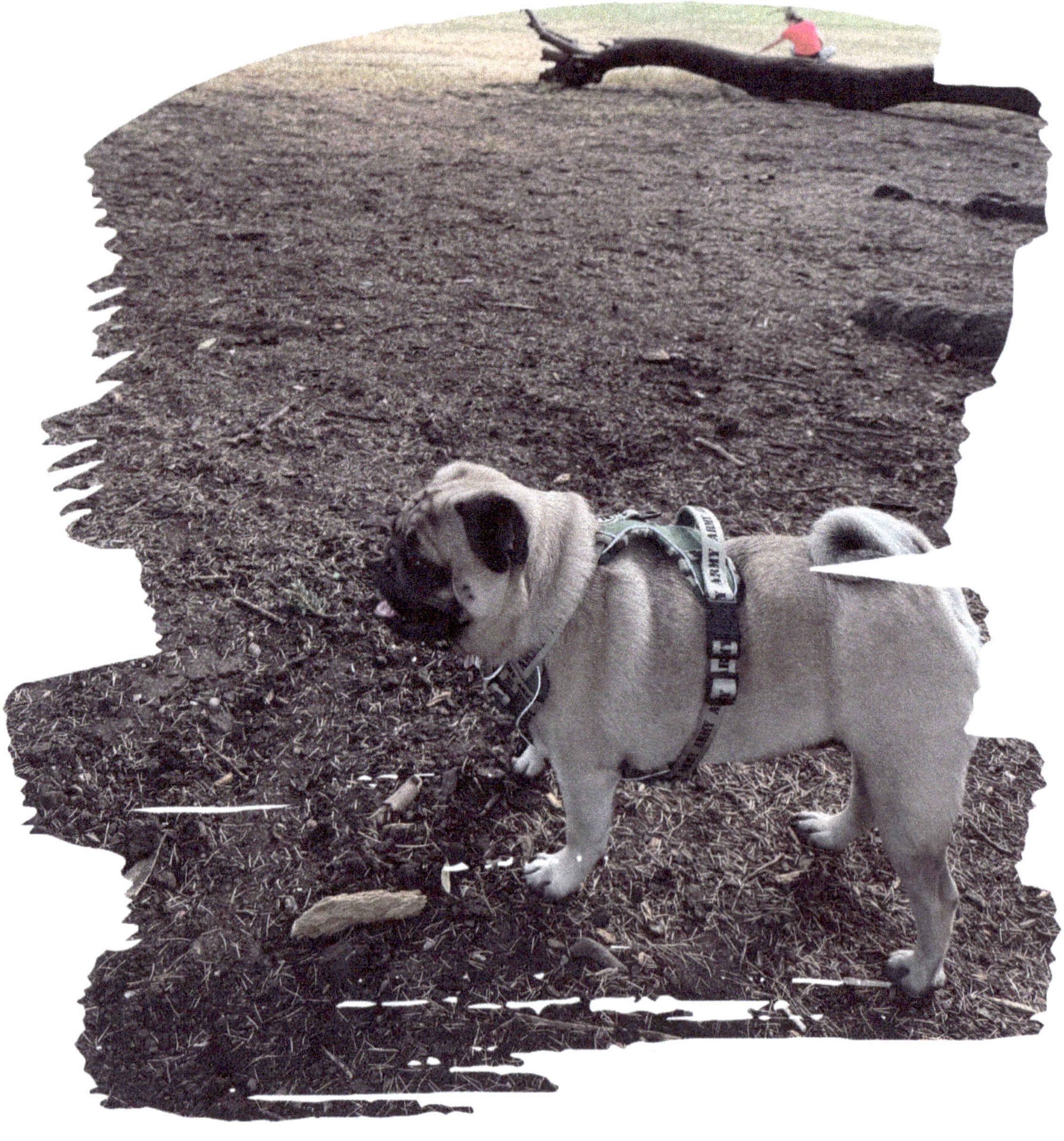

The Walk-Away Wisdom

Phil-osophical Quote:

"If they make you shrink, walk away. Even if you loved them once. Some dogs wag once and vanish. That's not your fault."

From Phil's Heart:

I met a spaniel named Max. We sniffed. We played. We shared a stick. Next day? Nothing. Not even a glance. It stung. I've stayed too long. I've waited for kindness that never came. But I learned: not every wag means forever. Some are just passing breezes. You're allowed to feel it. You're allowed to let go. You're allowed to keep your softness intact. Walking away isn't weakness. It's wisdom. You're allowed to protect your softness. You're allowed to leave.

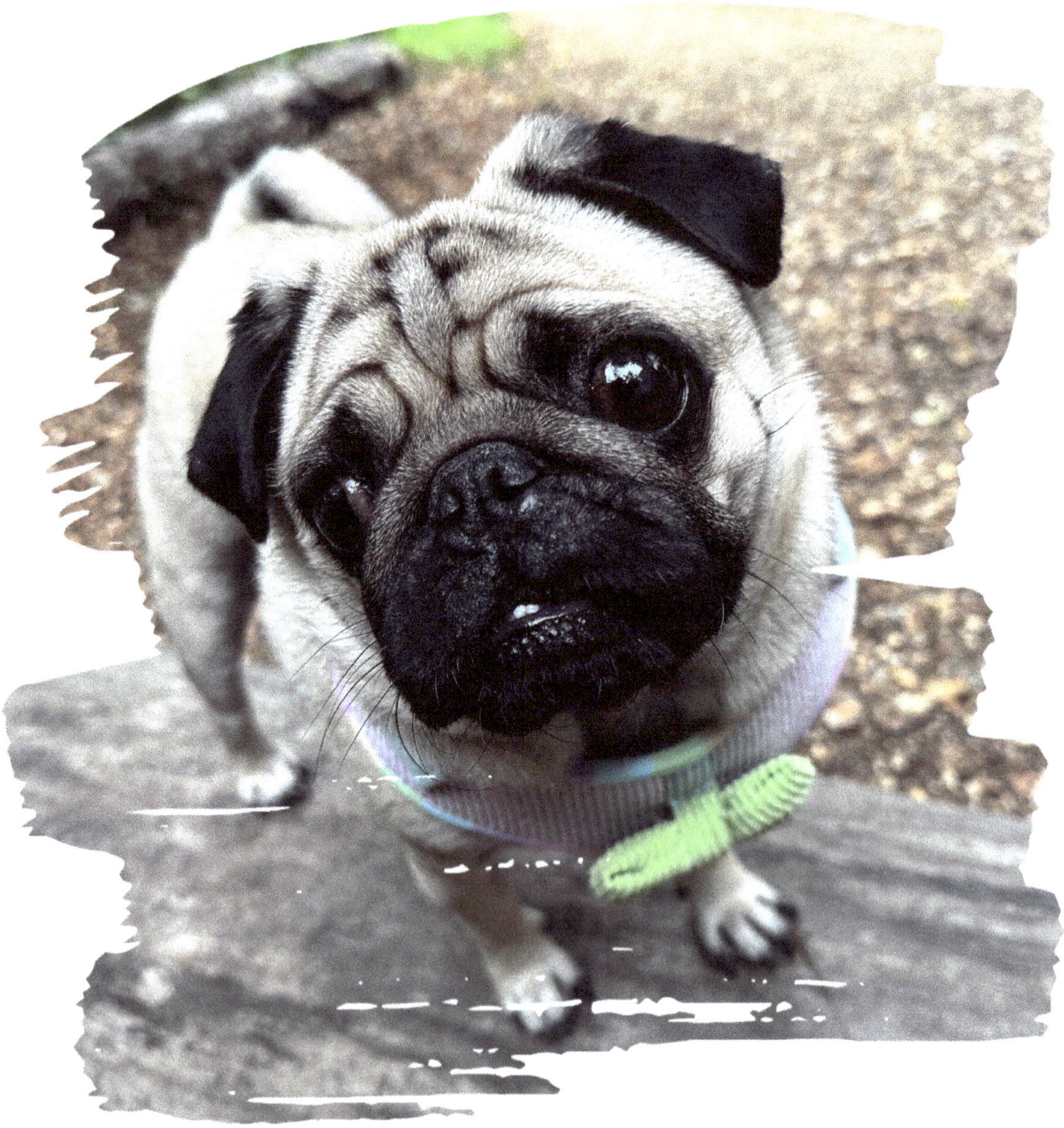

🧠 Phil's Final Pawse

Phil-osophical Quote:

"You deserve to be seen. Not just looked at."

From Phil's Heart:

The good hoomans see past the fluff. They notice your quiet. They honour your weird. They don't just want your tricks. They want your truth. Find them. Follow them. And if you're lucky enough to be one—stay soft. Stay kind. Stay wag-worthy.

🐾 Chapter 9: The Ethics of Ear Licks & Emotional Labour

Affection is beautiful. But it's also effort. And effort deserves rest.

Welcome to Chapter nine. The one where we talk about love. Not the tail-wag kind. The effort kind.

I've licked ears that didn't deserve it. Sat beside sadness that never saw me. Offered comfort when I was the one who needed it.

This chapter is about emotional labour. The invisible kind. The kind that dogs do without asking. The kind that hoomans do too, sometimes without being thanked.

It's about knowing when to give. When to pause. And when to say, "I love you, but I need a nap."

The Unsolicited Ear Lick

Phil-osophical Quote:

"Sometimes you give comfort. Sometimes you just lick your own face."

From Phil's Heart:

I've licked ears that didn't ask for it. Offered comfort that wasn't returned. But this one time? I licked a pumpkin. Of myself. Because sometimes, the one who needs love... is you. And if that love comes with a snort and a tongue? So be it.

The Emotional Nap Clause

Phil-osophical Quote:

"Even the softest dogs need rest."

From Phil's Heart:

I'm known for my comfort. My presence. My snuggles. But sometimes, I hide under the blanket. Not because I'm sad. Because I'm tired. Emotional labour is real. And rest isn't selfish—it's sacred. Sometimes little bro George snuggles with me.

The Mutual Wag Agreement

Phil-osophical Quote:

"If you're always the one wagging... check the contract."

From Phil's Heart:

I've wagged for hoomans who never wagged back. I've comforted friends who never asked how I was. Affection should be mutual. Effort should be shared. If you're doing all the wagging—it's time to renegotiate.

The Juno Clause (Callback)

Phil-osophical Quote:

"Some dogs give too much. Until they find someone who gives back."

From Phil's Heart:

Juno used to lick everyone's ears. Even the ones who barked too loud. She gave and gave. Until she found her forever hooman. Now she naps more. Wags less. But when she does? It's real. She taught me that love isn't about effort. It's about safety.

🧠 Phil's Final Pawse

Phil-osophical Quote:

"You deserve love that doesn't exhaust you."

From Phil's Heart:

You're allowed to be tired. You're allowed to say no. You're allowed to ask for care. Affection is beautiful. But it's also work. And work needs rest. So, take your nap. Skip the ear lick. And wait for the ones who wag back.

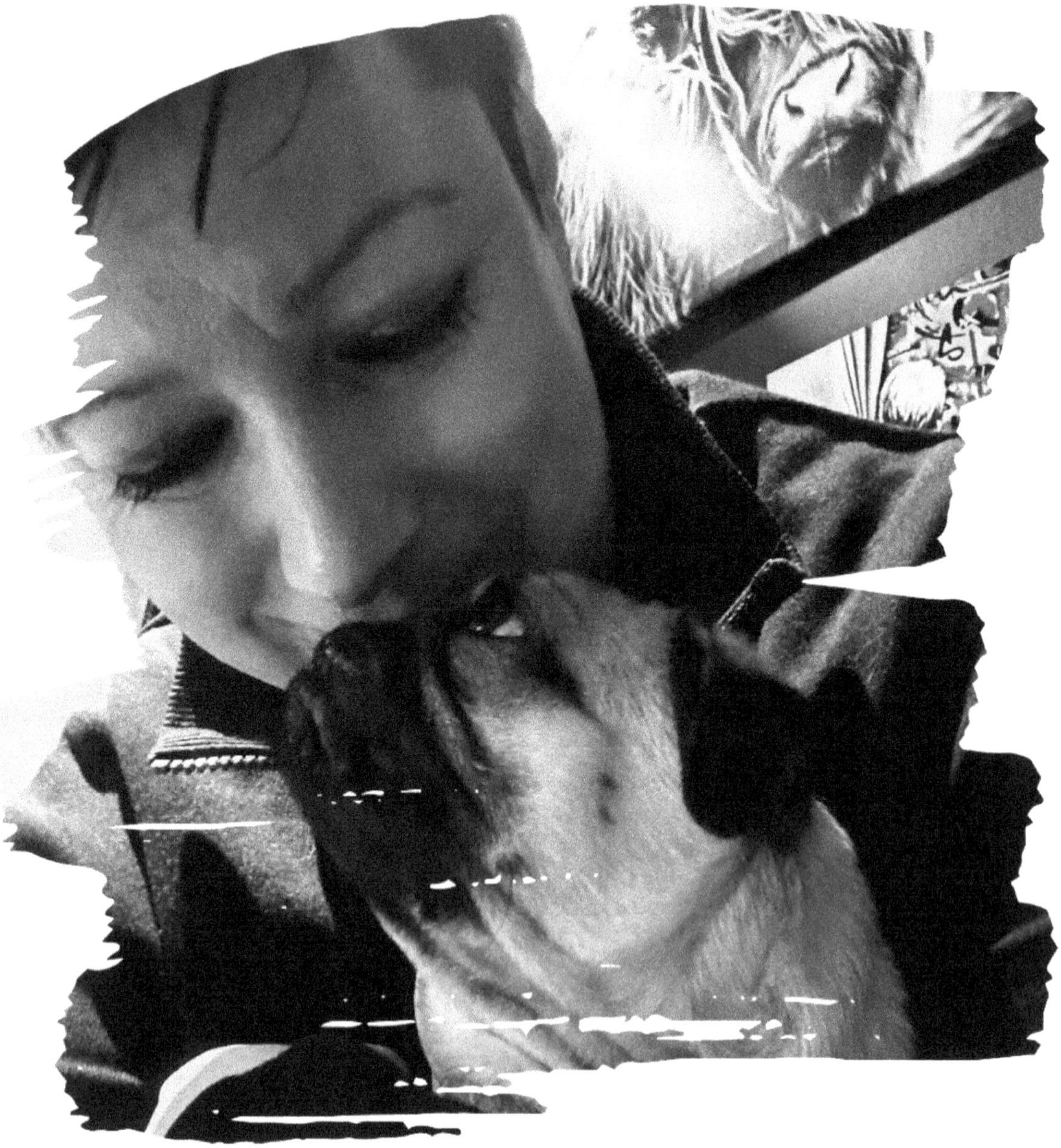

Chapter 10: Love Me, Love My Wiggle

Radical self-acceptance, tail-first

Welcome to Chapter Ten. Let's talk about the wiggle.

Not just the tail. The whole-body joy. The awkwardness. The snort-laced celebration of being exactly who you are.

I wiggle when I'm happy. I wiggle when I'm nervous. I wiggle when I don't know what else to do.

This chapter is about loving the wiggle. The weird. The wonderful. The parts of you that don't fit in but still deserve to be seen.

Love me, love my wiggle. Or kindly exit the park.

The Wiggle of Worry

Phil-osophical Quote:

"Even anxious wiggles deserve love."

From Phil's Heart:

Sometimes I wiggle when I'm unsure. When the park feels too big. When the hoomans are too loud. It's not a performance. It's a signal. And the ones who understand? They sit beside me. Quietly. Kindly.

The Wiggle of Weirdness

Phil-osophical Quote:

"Your weird is your wag."

From Phil's Heart:

I snort when I'm excited. I spin before I poop. I stare too long at nothing (possibly daydreaming – but still, it's been noticed). It's weird. It's wonderful. It's mine. And if you love me, you love all of it.

The Wiggle of Worth

Phil-osophical Quote:

"You don't have to shrink to be loved."

From Phil's Heart:

I used to think I had to be quiet. Small. Easy. But then I met hoomans who said, "Wiggle louder." Now I take up space. I snort freely. I wag like I mean it. Because love should never ask you to shrink.

🧠 Phil's Final Pawse

Phil-osophical Quote:

"Love me, love my wiggle. All of it."

From Phil's Heart:

You are not too much. You are just enough. Your wiggle is your truth. Your joy. Your signal to the world that you're alive and feeling. So wag it. Wiggle it. Own it. And find the ones who say, "I love that about you."

🐾 Chapter 11: Trust the Tail Wag

Instincts. Gut Feelings. Emotional Radar. Phil knows.

Welcome to Chapter eleven. Let's talk about trusting your feelings and snorting out the bad.

I don't always understand words. But I understand energy.

I know when a hooman's smile is hiding something. I know when a dog's bark means "stay back." I know when someone's heart is wagging, even if their face isn't.

This chapter is about trusting your tail. Your gut. Your emotional radar. Because sometimes, the wag knows before you do.

The Uneasy Wag

Phil-osophical Quote:

"If your tail hesitates... listen."

From Phil's Heart:

I've met hoomans who smiled too wide. Dogs who sniffed too fast. My tail didn't wag. Not fully. Just a twitch. That twitch was a warning. And I've learned to trust it.

The Full-Body Wag of Yes

Phil-osophical Quote:

"When it's right, your whole body knows."

From Phil's Heart:

Some hoomans walk in and I wag before I even see them. It's not logic. It's love. It's safety. It's truth. Your body knows. Your heart knows. Your tail knows.

The Ghost Wag

Phil-osophical Quote:

"Sometimes you wag for someone who's already gone."

From Phil's Heart:

I've waited at the door. Wagged for someone who never came back. It hurt. But it also meant I loved.

Even ghost wags matter. They remind us, we're capable of hope.

The Tail Wag Test

Phil-osophical Quote:

"If they pass the tail wag test... they're probably worth sniffing."

From Phil's Heart:

I don't wag for everyone. And that's okay. My tail is my truth. My boundary. My invitation. If it wags, I'm open. If it doesn't, I'm not. And that's emotional safety.

🧠 Phil's Final Pawse

Phil-osophical Quote:

"Your tail knows. Even when your heart's confused."

From Phil's Heart:

Trust the twitch. Trust the wag. Trust the stillness. Your body is wise. Your instincts are kind. And if someone makes you wag without trying? Keep them.

Chapter 12: The Emotional Leash Agreement

Boundaries, trust, and walking together—even when the lead is invisible

Welcome to my final chapter. Chapter twelve. Let's talk about presence, trust, and quiet companionship because some bonds don't need a lead. Just love.

I don't wear a leash in the park. I don't need to.

I stay close. I listen. I trust. And they trust me.

This chapter isn't about leads. It's about loyalty. It's about knowing when to walk together, when to pause, and when to zoom.

It's about emotional boundaries—the kind you don't see but feel. It's about the leash you don't need when love is enough.

The Invisible Lead

Phil-osophical Quote:

"If they stay close without being pulled... that's real."

From Phil's Heart:

I walk beside them. Not because I have to. Because I want to. The good hoomans don't yank. They invite. And I follow—not out of fear, but out of love.

The Zoomie Clause

Phil-osophical Quote:

"Freedom is knowing you can run – but still be found."

From Phil's Heart:

Sometimes I zoom. Fast. Wild. Free. But I always come back. Because I know where safety lives. The emotional leash isn't about control. It's about trust. And trust means you can run without getting lost.

The Pause Agreement

Phil-osophical Quote:

"If they wait when you stop... they're walking with you, not ahead of you."

From Phil's Heart:

I pause sometimes. To sniff. To think. To feel. And they wait. No tug. No rush. That's how I know we're walking together—not just in the same direction, but at the same pace.

The Emotional Lead

"Some bonds are felt, not fastened."

From Phil's Heart:

I've seen dogs pulled too hard. Rushed. Ignored. But I've also seen the quiet ones. The ones who walk side by side, no lead, just love. That's the kind of leash I believe in. The kind that says: "I trust you. Come with me.

🧠 Phil's Final Pawse

Phil-osophical Quote:

"Love is the leash you don't feel – but always follow."

From Phil's Heart:

You don't need to be pulled to be close. You don't need to be held to be safe. The best walks are the ones where you're free—and still choose to stay. That's love. That's trust. That's the emotional leash agreement.

Bonus Section

🧠 Final Pawse: What Phil Wants You to Remember

"You are wag-worthy. Always."

- Your softness is not a flaw. It's your superpower.
- You don't have to shrink to be loved.
- Some tail wags are earned. Some aren't. Know the difference.
- Comfort is a gift. But it's okay to keep some for yourself.
- Your weird is your wag. Own it.
- The best walks are the ones where you're free—and still choose to stay.
- Even ghost wags matter. They mean you cared.
- You deserve love that doesn't exhaust you.
- Trust the twitch. Trust the wag. Trust the stillness.
- If someone makes you wag without trying... keep them.

And if you ever forget any of this—just look at Phil. He remembers for *you.*

🧠 Phil's Emotional Survival Kit

For when the world feels too loud, too heavy, or just too much.

"You don't need to fix everything. You just need a safe spot to snort."
—Phil

🐾 Phil's Essentials for Emotional Survival

Item	Why It Helps
A Soft Blanket	For wrapping yourself in safety. Bonus if it smells like someone who loves you.
A Biscuit You Don't Have to Share	Because comfort shouldn't come with conditions.
A Quiet Corner	Not isolation—sanctuary. A place to breathe, nap, or just exist.
A Trusted Hooman	Someone who doesn't ask questions when you snort-cry.
A Tail Wag Trigger	Ducks, zoomies, or a squeaky toy—whatever reminds you joy still exists.
Permission to Nap	Emotional labour is exhausting. Rest is resistance.
A Sniff of Something Familiar	Nostalgia is grounding. Even if it's just your old slipper.
A Pawprint Reminder	You've made an impact. Even if you can't see it yet.
A Safe Word (or Snort)	Something that says "I need space" without needing to explain.
A Mirror That Doesn't Judge	For looking at yourself and saying, "Still here. Still wag-worthy."

✍️ Build Your Own Kit

Fill in the blanks with your own emotional essentials. Phil approves.

- My comfort object: _____

- My safe hooman: _____

- My tail-wag trigger: _____

- My emotional nap spot: _____

- My reminder that I matter: _____

"Whatever's in your kit, make sure it includes kindness. Especially for yourself." —Phil

📖 Phil's Emotional Glossary

A snort-to-tail guide to Phil's emotional language.

"Words are useful. But snorts? Snorts are truth." —Phil

🐾 Phil-isms and What They Mean

Term	Definition
Ghost Wag	A tail wag for someone who's gone. A sign of lingering love or hope.
Snort Pause	A moment of emotional overwhelm. Often followed by a nap or biscuit.
Blanket Trust	The kind of safety that lets you nap without checking the exits.
Zoomie Clause	The emotional freedom to run wild knowing you'll still be welcomed back.
Ear Lick Effort	Unseen emotional labour. Comforting others even when you're tired.
Tail Wag Test	Phil's method of assessing emotional safety. If the tail wags, proceed.
Emotional Leash Agreement	A mutual bond built on trust, not control. No tugging allowed.
Wiggle of Worth	A full-body celebration of being exactly who you are.
Boundary Biscuit	A treat you don't share. A metaphor for emotional limits.
Snuggle Consent	The unspoken agreement that cuddles are mutual, not expected.
Park Philosophy	The belief that everyone deserves space, respect, and a good sniff.
Forever Friend Criteria	Loyalty, kindness, and biscuit-worthiness. Phil-approved.

"If you don't know what to say, try a snort. It usually works." —Phil

🐾 Phil's Forever Friend Contract

A gentle agreement between you and the ones who walk beside you

"Good hoomans don't tug. They wait. They wag. They walk with you." —Phil

✍️ Your Emotional Leash Agreement

Fill this out when you're ready to walk with someone who sees your wiggle and says, *"I love that about you."*

I feel safe when:

My emotional zoomies look like:

People I trust to walk beside me:

If I pause, I need them to:

☐ Wait quietly

☐ Offer a biscuit

☐ Sit beside me

☐ Say "Take your time"

☐ Other: _____

My tail wags for:

My emotional boundaries include:

☐ Saying no without guilt

☐ Napping when I'm tired

☐ Not licking ears I don't want to

☐ Only sharing my blanket with safe hoomans

☐ Other: _____

Signed:

(Your name, your pawprint, or your snort)

> ***"You deserve a leash made of love. Not rope." —Phil***

🐶 Meet Phil the Pug

Snort ambassador. Emotional Support Specialist. Blanket Thief.

"I'm not just a pug. I'm a phil-osophy." —Phil

Full Name	Phil (just Phil—no middle name, no nonsense)
Breed	Pug, obviously. Compact, snorty, emotionally fluent.
Age	Timeless. But also… whatever age makes him wise and snack-worthy. (I'm 2 years old, shhh).
Favourite Snack	Anything that isn't his prescription kibble.
Signature Move	The slow approach, the deep stare, and the sudden snort.
Emotional Superpower	Knowing when someone needs a nap—even before they do.
Zoomie Frequency	Occasional. But when it happens, it's a full-body event.
Best Friend	Tina (his emotional anchor), Kaz (his creative translator), and George (his chaos apprentice).
Known For	Licking a pumpkin of his own face. And making people cry in a good way.

🐾 Phil's Top 5 Life Lessons

1. *If you're tired, nap. If you're sad, snort. If you're loved, stay close.*
2. *Not everyone deserves your ear lick. Save it for the biscuit-worthy.*
3. *You don't have to be loud to be heard. Just present.*
4. *Zoomies are sacred. Don't apologise for joy.*
5. *Love me, love my wiggle. Or kindly exit the park.*

💬 Phil's Voice in the Book

Phil's words are soft, snorty, and full of emotional truth. He doesn't bark—he reflects. He doesn't chase—he chooses. And every chapter in this book is a tribute to the quiet power of being exactly who you are.

"I didn't ask to be wise. I just listened. And snorted. And stayed." —
Phil

💌 About the Author: Kaz's Journey

Creative. Resilient. Wag-Worthy.

"I didn't write this book because I had all the answers. I wrote it because I needed them too." —Kaz

There was a time when the world felt heavy. When joy was something I had to chase, not something that came naturally. I've lived with depression. I've known the weight of days that don't make sense. I've felt the ache of trying to be okay— for others, for myself, for the pets who needed me.

And then there was Phil.

Phil didn't fix everything. But he reminded me that softness is strength. That snorts are valid. That naps are sacred. He stayed close when I couldn't explain why I needed him. He wagged when I couldn't. He became my emotional anchor, my creative muse, and my reason to write something that might help someone else feel seen.

This book isn't just a tribute to Phil. It's a love letter to anyone who's ever felt too much, too little, or too lost. It's a reminder that emotional survival doesn't have to be loud. It can be gentle. It can be snorty. It can be a quiet walk beside someone who understands.

I'm Kaz. I live in West London with Tina, Ezra, George, Phil, Zachary, and Saffron. I write stories that comfort. I design things that hug. I believe in emotional literacy, radical softness, and the healing power of pet birthday cards.

If you're reading this, thank you. You're part of Phil's universe now. And that means you're wag-worthy too.

🧠 Things That Helped Me Heal

- Creating rituals that made me feel safe
  - Writing from Phils' perspective

- Celebrating small wins (like a good cup of tea or a successful delivery)
  - Letting myself be loved, even when I didn't feel lovable
  - Remembering that softness isn't weakness—it's wisdom

🙏 Acknowledgments

For every smile, hug, and quiet moment of support

To **Tina**, my anchor, my co-wiggler, my heart. You've held me through the hard days, laughed with me through the weird ones, and loved me exactly as I am. Every page of this book carries your warmth.

To **Ezra**, whose quiet strength and fierce love inspire me daily. You remind me that softness and courage can live in the same heart, no matter how young you are.

To **George**, the newest furbaby in our family. You've already taught me so much about joy, chaos, and unconditional love.

To **Zachary & Saffron**, our feline royalty. You bring drama, dignity, and the kind of emotional depth only cats can offer.

To **Phil**, the soul behind every word. You didn't just inspire this book—you saved me. You reminded me that emotional survival can be gentle, funny, and full of love. You are my muse, my mirror, and my emotional translator.

To everyone who's ever read a chapter, shared a post, or whispered "me too" while holding this book, or any others of ours—thank you. You are part of Phil's universe now. And that means you're wag-worthy.

To those who walk beside me creatively, emotionally, and spiritually—thank you for letting me pause, reflect, and move at my own pace without judgment.

And finally, to anyone who's ever felt too much, too little, or too lost: **this book is for you**. May it be your comfort, your safe space, your quiet reminder that **you're not alone**.

🌐 Stay Connected: Phil's World Online

Because emotional support doesn't end at the last page.

"If you liked this book, you'll love the rest of my stories." —Phil

🐾 Find Phil Online

- **Website: www.philthepug.com** - *Books, merch, updates, and emotional resources—all in one place*
- **Instagram: @phil_the_pug_star** - *Photos, quotes, zoomies, and behind-the-scenes snorts*
- **TikTok: @philthepug -** *Short videos, emotional pep talks, and Phil's wisdom*

📚 Phil's Books So Far

Phil the Pug – *The Puppy Chronicles* (Phil's 1st Memoir)

Phil the Pug – *Born to be a Legend* (Phil's 2nd Memoir)

Phil the Pug – *Phil and the Cat who Almost Liked Him*

Phil the Pug – *Phil and the Big Back-to-School Snuffle*

Phil the Pug – *Phil and the Pug Phlip: The Match that Mattered*

Phil the Pug – *Phil and the Rise of the Vampire Pug: A Halloween Tale*

Books That Hug Back

Kaz
&Pug
PRESS

a PhilKaz imprint

www.ingramcontent.com/pod-product-compliance
Lightning Source LLC
Chambersburg PA
CBHW040300100426
42811CB00011B/1323